The MIRACLES of ARCHANGEL GABRIEL

Also by Doreen Virtue

Books/Calendar/Kits/Oracle Board

Assertiveness for Earth Angels (available November 2013)
How to Heal a Grieving Heart (with James Van Praag; available October 2013)
Whispers from Above 2014 Calendar (available September 2013)
Mermaids 101
Flower Therapy (with Robert Reeves)
Mary, Queen of Angels
Saved by an Angel
The Angel Therapy® Handbook
Angel Words (with Grant Virtue)
Archangels 101
The Healing Miracles of Archangel Raphael
The Art of Raw Living Food (with Jenny Ross)
Signs from Above (with Charles Virtue)
The Miracles of Archangel Michael
Angel Numbers 101
Solomon's Angels (a novel)
My Guardian Angel (with Amy Oscar)
Angel Blessings Candle Kit (with Grant Virtue; includes booklet, CD, journal, etc.)
Thank You, Angels! (children's book with Kristina Tracy)
Healing Words from the Angels
How to Hear Your Angels
Realms of the Earth Angels
Fairies 101
Daily Guidance from Your Angels
Divine Magic
How to Give an Angel Card Reading Kit
Angels 101
Angel Guidance Board
Goddesses & Angels
Crystal Therapy (with Judith Lukomski)
Connecting with Your Angels Kit (includes booklet, CD, journal, etc.)
Angel Medicine
The Crystal Children
Archangels & Ascended Masters
Earth Angels
Messages from Your Angels
Angel Visions II
Eating in the Light (with Becky Prelitz, M.F.T., R.D.)
The Care and Feeding of Indigo Children
Healing with the Fairies
Angel Visions
Divine Prescriptions
Healing with the Angels
"I'd Change My Life If I Had More Time"
Divine Guidance
Chakra Clearing
Angel Therapy®
The Lightworker's Way
Constant Craving A–Z
Constant Craving
The Yo-Yo Diet Syndrome
Losing Your Pounds of Pain

Audio/CD Programs

Angel Therapy® Meditations
Archangels 101 (abridged audio book)
Fairies 101 (abridged audio book)
Goddesses & Angels (abridged audio book)
Angel Medicine (available as both 1- and 2-CD sets)
Angels among Us (with Michael Toms)
Messages from Your Angels (abridged audio book)
Past-Life Regression with the Angels
Divine Prescriptions
The Romance Angels
Connecting with Your Angels
Manifesting with the Angels
Karma Releasing
Healing Your Appetite, Healing Your Life
Healing with the Angels
Divine Guidance
Chakra Clearing

DVD Program

How to Give an Angel Card Reading

Oracle Cards (divination cards and guidebook)

Talking to Heaven Mediumship Cards (with James Van Praagh;
available November 2013)
Archangel Power Tarot Cards (with Radleigh Valentine; available October 2013)
Flower Therapy Oracle Cards (with Robert Reeves; available September 2013)
Indigo Angel Oracle Cards (with Charles Virtue)
Angel Dreams Oracle Cards (with Melissa Virtue)
Mary, Queen of Angels Oracle Cards
Angel Tarot Cards (with Radleigh Valentine and Steve A. Roberts)
The Romance Angels Oracle Cards
Life Purpose Oracle Cards
Archangel Raphael Healing Oracle Cards
Archangel Michael Oracle Cards
Angel Therapy® Oracle Cards
Magical Messages from the Fairies Oracle Cards
Ascended Masters Oracle Cards
Daily Guidance from Your Angels Oracle Cards
Saints & Angels Oracle Cards
Magical Unicorns Oracle Cards
Goddess Guidance Oracle Cards
Archangel Oracle Cards
Magical Mermaids and Dolphins Oracle Cards
Messages from Your Angels Oracle Cards
Healing with the Fairies Oracle Cards
Healing with the Angels Oracle Cards

All of the above are available at your
local bookstore, or may be ordered by visiting:

Hay House USA: **www.hayhouse.com**®
Hay House Australia: **www.hayhouse.com.au**
Hay House UK: **www.hayhouse.co.uk**
Hay House South Africa: **www.hayhouse.co.za**
Hay House India: **www.hayhouseco.in**

Doreen's website: **www.AngelTherapy.com**

ANNUNCIATION

The MIRACLES *of* ARCHANGEL GABRIEL

DOREEN VIRTUE

HAY HOUSE, INC.
Carlsbad, California • New York City
London • Sydney • Johannesburg
Vancouver • Hong Kong • New Delhi

Published and distributed in the United States by: Hay House, Inc.:
www.hayhouse.com • *Published and distributed in Australia by:*
Hay House Australia Pty. Ltd.: www.hayhouse.com.au • *Published
and distributed in the United Kingdom by:* Hay House UK, Ltd.:
www.hayhouse.co.uk • *Published and distributed in the Republic
of South Africa by:* Hay House SA (Pty), Ltd.: www.hayhouse.co.za
• *Distributed in Canada by:* Raincoast: www.raincoast.com • *Published in India by:* Hay House Publishers India: www.hayhouse.co.in

Cover and interior design: Tricia Breidenthal

Library of Congress Cataloging-in-Publication Data

Virtue, Doreen.
   THE MIRACLES OF ARCHANGEL GABRIEL / Doreen Virtue. -- 1st ed.
      pages cm
   ISBN 978-1-4019-2636-6 (hardcover : alk. paper) 1. Gabriel
(Archangel)--Miscellanea. 2. Miracles. I. Title.
   BL477.V575 2013
   202'.15--dc23

Hardcover ISBN: 978-1-4019-2636-6
Digital ISBN: 978-1-4019-3630-3

16 15 14 13   4 3 2 1
1st edition, July 2013

Printed in China

To Our Blessed
Mother Mary

Contents

Introduction

*"Fear not: for, behold, I bring you
good tidings of great joy . . ."*

These poetic words from Archangel Gabriel during the Annunciation of Mary's motherhood (Luke 2:10) stir great emotion within me and many others. This sentence is Gabriel's heralding of the news of the forthcoming birth of a true miracle worker. What a powerful message to bring to Earth!

In this nondenominational book, we'll study Gabriel, the messenger angel. Gabriel continues to be a messenger for mothers, writers, and artists everywhere, as you'll read in the true stories within these pages.

Just to clarify, I don't advocate the worship of angels, or even praying to them. Angels don't want to be worshipped. Instead, all glory is given to God, the Creator of angels and of all of us. This book explores how God sends angels to those in need. In particular, Archangel Gabriel is assigned to help mothers and messengers.

The History and Symbols of Archangel Gabriel

Along with Michael, Gabriel is one of the only two named angels in the *canonical* Bible, which is a term describing the Bible accepted by most Christian faiths. Some religions approve of additional sacred books (usually the Dead Sea Scrolls) as part of their Bible, and those describe the other archangels. For example, the archangel Raphael was named in the deuterocanonical Book of Tobit (recognized by Catholic, Eastern Orthodox, and Oriental Orthodox faiths), and Uriel only appears in Apocryphal biblical books. Archangel Metatron is described in the Book of Enoch, another Dead Sea Scroll.

Although Michael and Gabriel are named in the canonical Bible, only Gabriel has conversations and encounters with people. In all sacred books featuring Gabriel, this angel is busily interacting with and delivering guidance to people. As you'll see in this book, Gabriel continues to actively interact engage with individuals of all walks of life.

Gabriel's name means "God's strength" or "Strength of God," derived from the Semitic root *geber,* which means "to be strong" or "to use more power," and *el,* which means "God" or "of God." Gabriel is mostly known as the "Messenger Angel." Since the word *angel* means "Messenger of God," Gabriel is thought to be the overseer of human and angelic messengers. And since the prefix *arch-* means "first" or "chief," Gabriel is the "First or Chief Messenger." In fact, Gabriel *is* the first named angel in the Bible (in the Book of Daniel). Gabriel is an important angel in the three monotheistic religions of Judaism, Christianity, and Islam.

Gabriel is initially mentioned in the Dead Sea Scroll Book of Daniel. Scholars agree that the Book of Daniel was written in the 2nd century, and consists of a blend of written traditions, an analysis of the history of Babylon, and prophetic visions. These visions and dreams were from the Babylonian king and from Daniel, who worked for the king as an official dream interpreter. Archangel Gabriel plays an active role in helping Daniel interpret these visions, including his prophecy about the coming Messiah. Most believe Daniel's Messiah prophecy to be about Jesus Christ, based upon the timeline and other details contained in it.

Archangel Gabriel's next appearance is in the Book of Luke, which is the longest book in the synoptic New Testament Gospels (the books of Matthew, Mark, and Luke, which describe the same Bible stories in different ways ["synoptically"]).

Luke is believed to have been a physician and follower of Apostle Paul, who lived and wrote the Gospel in the Greek language nearly 100 years after Jesus's ascension. He is the only Gospel author to call Archangel Gabriel by name.

Luke first describes Gabriel's encounter with Zechariah, an elderly priest. Both Zechariah and his wife, Elizabeth, were descendants of Aaron, who was Moses's older brother. Zechariah and Elizabeth were childless, and beyond childbearing years. So Zechariah was afraid and surprised when he saw Archangel Gabriel in the temple where he worked. Gabriel said to him:

> Fear not, Zacharias: for thy prayer is heard; and thy wife Elisabeth shall bear thee a son, and thou shalt call his name John. And thou shalt have joy and gladness; and many shall rejoice at his birth. For he shall be great in the sight of

the Lord, and shall drink neither wine nor strong drink; and he shall be filled with the Holy Ghost, even from his mother's womb. And many of the children of Israel shall he turn to the Lord their God (Luke 1:13–16).

At first, Zechariah argued with the angel, saying that he and his wife were too old to have children. But soon after, the angel's prophecy came true and Elizabeth conceived and gave birth to a son, who would be known as John the Baptist.

Six months later, Gabriel delivered a similar Annunciation to Mary, wife of Joseph, about the forthcoming birth of Jesus Christ. Mary was also surprised by this prophecy, since she was still a virgin. Yet, just as with Zechariah and Elizabeth's unlikely conception, so too did Gabriel's prophecy for Mary prove true. Since Archangel Gabriel had assisted the prophet Daniel in interpreting his vision about the coming Messiah, the angel was actually involved in *two* annunciations proclaiming Jesus's arrival.

Six hundred years after Jesus's mortal life, the prophet Mohammed of the Arabian Mekkah (today known as Mecca) was visited by Archangel Gabriel while he was meditating in a cave. Mohammed continued receiving revelations from the angel until the end of his life. Mohammed's written revelations from Gabriel are the Islamic scripture, the Koran or Qur'an. In it, the archangel is referred to as Jibril, which is the Arabic translation of Gabriel.

In the book *Mohammed: The Man and His Faith* by T. Andrae, the author quotes Mohammed describing his interactions with Archangel Gabriel:

The revelation comes to me in two ways. Sometimes Gabriel visits me and tells it to me as though one man were speaking to another, but then what he speaks is lost to me. But sometimes it comes to me as with the noise of a bell, so that my heart is confused. But what is revealed to me in this way never leaves me.

Gabriel is also described in the Books of Enoch, sacred Dead Sea Scrolls that comprise three canonical books of the Ethiopian Orthodox Church and the Eritrean Orthodox Tewahedo Church. Enoch was the great-grandfather of Noah and the great-grandson of Adam, who visited heaven with the help of archangels Gabriel and Michael, and had clear glimpses of God and the angels. At the end of his life, God transformed Enoch into the archangel Metatron.

In the first Book of Enoch, Archangel Gabriel is summoned by God to banish the Watchers (fallen angels who paired with human women to produce children) and sinners from the world. The book also describes Gabriel as "one of the holy angels who oversees the Garden of Eden, the serpents, and the cherubim" (1 Enoch 20:7).

Gabriel also plays significant roles in Hebrew *midrashims* (legends and writings that expand upon the Hebrew Bible stories). According to the midrashims,

Gabriel was responsible for helping baby Abraham stay alive; taught languages to Joseph; and caused baby Moses to cry in order to attract the attention of the Pharaoh's daughter, who then adopted him.

Gabriel's Symbols: Lilies and a Horn

Each archangel has a symbol that signifies a specific mission. For example, Archangel Michael has a sword because he triumphs over fear. Raphael's symbol is a fish, because the Book of Tobit describes how the angel healed a blind man by putting ground-up fish in his eyes (along with offering healing prayers).

Gabriel's symbols are a copper horn and white lily flowers. Gabriel uses the horn to herald messages and gain our attention. Some people believe that Gabriel's horn will also be used for a "Judgment Day," although this is a legend that began centuries after the Bible was written, in popular literature such as *Paradise Lost* by John Milton and artwork dating back to at least the 1400s.

Gabriel is usually portrayed holding a long stem of white lilies, as in the painting on the facing page.

Lilies represent purity and spiritual faith. They are also associated with Mother Mary's humility, so Gabriel carries lilies as a symbolic connection to the Blessed Mother. Lilies with three petals are symbolic of the Holy Trinity, and are the basis of the *fleur-de-lis*.

A reader named Michele Lackey told me her story of Gabriel and this special flower:

> Rather late one night I stopped at the grocery store. I'd been going through a stressful time of transition from my last assignment working at a yoga retreat center. I was confused and unsure what would happen next with my career.

It was the time of night when the coffee section was closed and all the chairs were up on the tables.

Suddenly I stopped. There, draped across one of the tables, was a long-stem lily of the valley—the same type of flower pictured with Gabriel in so many portraits!

I wondered how it got there as I went to the cashier to pay for my items. (By the way, I didn't pick it up because I thought they might think I stole it from the flower section. Honestly, the mundane mind can be such a bummer sometimes!) While I was in line, I decided I'd get it on my way out. But when I went back, it was gone! It all seemed so mysterious.

Now I don't know what happened with the flower, but ever since then the lily of the valley has become sacred to me. Every time I see the flower, I feel an especially strong connection with it. Now I also use it in my healing-flower meditations to great effect. In addition, I'm reminded every time of Archangel Gabriel. I'm so thankful for that event, because it has gifted me many times over with a felt sense of Divine Presence.

Although the Bible never mentions Gabriel holding a horn, this instrument has become a literary and artistic symbol of the archangel heralding a message. Because Gabriel appears in two apocalyptic scriptural books (the Book of Daniel and the Book of Enoch, with both describing historical apocalyptic events relevant to those times, such as the fall of Babylon), many have concluded that Gabriel's horn will blow to signal the "end times." This belief is also described in Hebrew midrashims.

This seems like a dark interpretation of the horn, which is more likely used to get people's attention so that they'll listen to the forthcoming message! In truth, Gabriel plays a larger role in announcing new *beginnings* (with John the Baptist's and Jesus Christ's births) than in end-time prophecy.

Regarding Gabriel's Gender

Controversy and speculation surround Gabriel's gender identity. Is Gabriel a male or a female angel? The Old and New Testament Bible, Koran, and Dead Sea Scrolls describe Gabriel with male pronouns. Yet countless paintings of the Annunciation give Gabriel a female face and body and feminine clothing. Just notice the paintings of Gabriel in this book and you'll see the angel wearing a flowing gown and with long, wavy hair. Contrast this to the paintings of Archangel Michael, who is always portrayed with ultra-masculine features, armor, and bulging muscles.

Ultimately, the angels don't have human bodies with gender designations. However, they *do*

In most paintings and statues of the Annunciation, Gabriel is portrayed with feminine features and clothing.

have personalities and specialty roles that skew masculine or feminine.

Since angels are nonphysical, they can change their appearance so that we'll recognize them and not be afraid.

A woman from Copenhagen, Denmark, told me that when she was very ill and sitting in her doctor's waiting room, she felt a presence beside her. She looked up and saw a male angel next to her who said, "My name is Gabriel, and I am one of your guardian angels. Please don't be afraid about your health, as you will be completely cured. You have four spiritual helpers guarding you." He then showed the woman a vision of the four helpers. She felt calm and relieved, and very soon she was indeed well.

A few years later, she was in bed meditating when she saw a vision of a beautiful female angel, who also said her name was Gabriel. When asked why she'd previously appeared to her as a male angel, Gabriel relayed the information that "she" appeared as whichever gender best helps the person. The woman continues to receive help from Gabriel for her music and writing.

This is another example from someone who was surprised—and comforted—when Gabriel appeared to her in female form:

Following her divorce, Sabrina Mizerek was reestablishing her life. She'd had a miraculous experience during the divorce while praying for help, and witnessed the entire divorce proceedings go from contentious to being amicably resolved. So her spiritual path continued with her connecting with the archangels Michael and Gabriel.

Sabrina was surprised to read my writings about Gabriel being a feminine archangel. So she decided to ask Gabriel directly! She'd learned how to quiet her mind and focus upon asking for spiritual help. Sabrina prayed, closed her eyes, and silently said, *Archangel Gabriel, are you a feminine angel?*

She immediately heard a voice in her mind that sounded female, but not like her own female voice. The voice said *yes* in response to Sabrina's question. Sabrina became so excited upon hearing this answer so clearly that she almost lost her connection to Gabriel. But she tried her best to continue and decided to start writing

the thoughts and feelings that poured into her mind and filtered through her emotions.

Sabrina received the message from Gabriel that she, Sabrina, was a strong woman, a warrior of love like the archangel. The angel communicated through thoughts and feelings that it was time for Sabrina to put her dreams into action, and to spend more time playing with her young son, as well as listening to him more.

Sabrina's connection with Gabriel has strengthened, and she's moved forward with her parenting and with her dreams. She says, "I feel much gratitude and very blessed."

You'll notice that the stories in this book contain both male and female pronouns for Archangel Gabriel, according to the perception of the person relaying the experience. Always, there is a great respect for the Bible, tradition, and the archangel of the Annunciation.

Perhaps with religion being predominantly patriarchal, Archangel Gabriel seeks to balance the male and female energies for those who need feminine strength and comforting. After all, Gabriel is most closely associated with the Queen of the Angels, Mother Mary, who is also the embodiment of ideal femininity paired with supreme strength.

I find that Archangel Gabriel offers perfectly balanced patriarchal and matriarchal support to those who encounter this powerful angel. Gabriel is both nurturing, kind, compassionate, and gentle (considered feminine properties) *and* also strong, supportive, and motivational (considered male properties).

In the end, any controversy about Archangel Gabriel's gender is dispelled by a focus upon this glorious angel's help and healing offered to us all. The stories within this book are remarkable, poignant, and impressive.

If you've read my other books in the *Miracles* series (*The Miracles of Archangel Michael, The Healing Miracles of Archangel Raphael,* and *Mary, Queen of Angels*), then you'll be able to feel the energetic differences within them.

Archangel Michael's strong and very male energy has a palpable physical heat associated with his presence. Many people actually perspire when they call upon or encounter him.

Archangel Raphael's energy is very gentle and feels like a soft healing vibration reverberating throughout the person who receives a healing from him.

The Blessed Mother Mary brings an otherworldly sweetness, purity, and graciousness, combined with clear and strong boundaries, as the ideal mother who loves her children completely but also is stern when necessary in order to keep them safe.

Since Archangel Gabriel is so connected to Mother Mary, it makes sense that this angel would share a similar balance of soft and strong energies.

In Chapter 1, we'll explore how Archangel Gabriel helps mothers and allows babies to enter this world upon the wings of angels.

Chapter One

CONCEPTION AND PREGNANCY

When Archangel Gabriel announced to Zechariah that his wife, Elizabeth, would give birth to a son who would be the predecessor of Jesus Christ, the priest was skeptical. After all, he and his wife were of advanced years. Many scholars believe Elizabeth was beyond childbearing age. Yet, as described in the Introduction, Gabriel's announcement proved true, and she gave birth to John the Baptist, who would travel to various cities prior to Jesus.

Probably the most famous Annunciation occurred when Archangel Gabriel visited Mary to proclaim that she'd give birth to a son named Jesus Christ. Just as Zechariah was incredulous at this news, so too was Mary, who was still a virgin.

Ever since Gabriel's announcement about the births of John the Baptist and Jesus Christ, the archangel has been associated with the news of conception. While one might think that visitations by an important angel such as Gabriel would be reserved for saints, myriad stories show that the archangel helps pure-hearted parents everywhere. Archangel Gabriel's announcements of miraculous births continue to this day, as you'll read in this chapter.

For example, a woman named Venyz from Malaysia received a message from Archangel Gabriel in a dream. In it, Venyz was kneeling with head bowed in front of a masculine angel with golden curly hair. He was wearing a gold-colored robe with sparkly light surrounding him. He looked almost translucent.

Venyz immediately knew that it was Archangel Gabriel who was standing in front of her. He announced that she was pregnant, that God had sent her baby to her as a gift, and that she should take good care of him.

Venyz remembered feeling so curious about Archangel Gabriel at that point, because she wasn't entirely sure of the archangel's gender. But, as she recalled, "By that time I felt that I was floating up by the ceiling, and then I woke up."

She just assumed that it had all been a dream, but about a week later, she saw a doctor because of gastric pain, and he then confirmed that she was, in fact, pregnant. When she had an ultrasound not long after, she discovered that she was having a baby boy!

Venyz said, "I really thank God for giving me such a wonderful gift. My little son is about to turn two years old; and he is a smart, loving, easygoing boy!"

Venyz's story validates Gabriel's appearance in her dreams, because at the time, she wasn't even thinking of motherhood. This rules out the dream being the unconscious mind's creation, or the product of wishful thinking.

Many people have angelic visitations during their dreams, because their skeptical minds are asleep and their souls are open to spiritual contact. These visitations have a more-than-real quality to them, as compared to mere dreams. People who have visitations remember their details years after the experience, whereas dreams fade into distant memory over time.

Miscarriages are painful crises for mothers and their families, which produce deep grieving. Archangel Gabriel can be called upon to help heal the physical and emotional pain of miscarriages, as well as to calm the anxiety of pregnant mothers who have previously miscarried.

For example, a woman named Corinne told me about her profound experience involving Gabriel several years ago. At the time, she was 42 years old and had experienced two tragic miscarriages. She was pregnant again (just by several weeks) and understandably very nervous. To calm herself, she began to meditate by closing her eyes, breathing, and focusing upon

the Divine. One day during her meditation, Corinne saw a vision of Archangel Gabriel in her mind's eye.

Having had these mind's-eye visions myself since childhood, I can attest to their validity. Very often, I'll awaken from a dream with a clear vision that I can later substantiate through research or with an experience that happens as predicted. So I pay attention to other people's visions, too.

"In my mind's eye," Corinne recalled, "I saw Gabriel hand me a pink rose and give me a knowing smile. I knew from that point on that I was having a girl, that I would carry the pregnancy to completion, and that my baby would be under Gabriel's protection. Eight months later, I gave birth to an eight-pound, nine-ounce, perfect baby girl, whom I named Gabriela. Archangel Gabriel continues to watch out for my daughter, and we both feel very connected to him."

Sometimes, visions and dreams occur in combination so that mothers have both waking and sleeping visitations from Archangel Gabriel. This way, the mother has no doubt as to the heavenly origin of the messages about her forthcoming baby.

For an Angel Therapist™ named Camille Mojica Rey, Gabriel's visit came as a surprise. After all, Camille already had two children, and her husband didn't desire a third. Additionally, she'd suffered two miscarriages. Nonetheless, she felt a Divine nudging to have another child. But she worried that she was too old to conceive again.

Then one day, Camille had a vision of Archangel Gabriel, who appeared to her as a large female angel. Next, Camille had a dream of her mother holding a baby boy, and realized in the dream that it was her own child!

As Camille studied the story from the Gospel of Luke, she realized that Elizabeth was advanced in years when Gabriel announced her pregnancy. Biblical scholars believe that Elizabeth was postmenopausal and had never given birth prior to having her son, John the Baptist.

Camille was inspired to learn this! Very soon, she received confirmation that she was pregnant, and had the best and healthiest pregnancy ever.

Camille recently wrote to me, saying:

> I am happy to report that Lola Cristina Rey was born on Wednesday, September 26, 2012, at 12:19 P.M. in San Jose, California.
>
> The C-section went smoothly. Lola is healthy, and she was kicking even as the doctor made the incision to get her out. She is gorgeous and captured the hearts of all who came in contact with her in the hospital. She impressed even the doctors by smiling and tracking people with her eyes. "Didn't anyone tell her that babies don't do that at three days old?" quipped one doctor.
>
> The angels continued to watch over us in the hospital. I was reassured of this when we entered our "mother and baby" room and saw that it overlooked the hospital's chapel. From my bed,

I could see the steeple, beautiful redwood trees, and on Saturday night, the full moon rising.

Lola is named after my late mother. She looks just like the baby my mother showed me in the dream. I recently looked up the date of my first Gabriel visitation. It was October 15, 2011. Less than a year later, I have a new baby and a new career in which I am fulfilling my life purpose as a spiritual teacher. I will always have a special place in my heart for Archangel Gabriel for bringing me the news of these impending miracles.

Two thousand years after the biblical Annunciation, Archangel Gabriel continues to announce pregnancies to women around the world. Sometimes, Gabriel's announcement is about a current pregnancy, and other times it's about a future one. Either way, Gabriel's messages bring great joy to mothers, fathers, and their extended families.

I've noticed that many of the stories I receive about Archangel Gabriel announcing a forthcoming pregnancy involve meditation. This could be because meditation is the practice of quieting the mind and focusing upon God's will and messages. As people learn to ignore the noisy world and the sometimes-noisy inner chatter of the mind, they can better hear the Divine voice when it comes to every part of their lives.

It can seem challenging to learn to distinguish the true Divine voice from the imagination, the ego, or lower energies. However, just as with anything important, it requires practice—and what could be more important than learning how to clearly hear messages from God and the angels? The same skill also helps you hear guidance from Jesus, Mother Mary, and any other beloved deities of your religion.

You can take meditation classes, as a woman named Julie Lovelock did. She told me that this class led her to have a clear vision and message from Archangel Gabriel, announcing her pregnancy.

Julie had been through a particularly difficult period in her life—she'd had issues with her mother, her ex-husband, and a very ill son, and had suffered from deep

depression. Then she met a wonderful man (her current husband, Gareth) who brought a lot of good into her life. For example, he would look after her son so that she could participate in a meditation circle.

During one meditation, Julie connected with angels and received guidance, but since she was a beginner, it was all very hazy. She did remember feeling a beautiful, warm, benevolent presence, and in her mind's eye, she could see a face that either nodded or shook its head when asked a question. Julie asked if she was pregnant, to which she received a nod. She then inquired if the baby would be a girl, and received another nod. Julie asked if the baby would be called Elizabeth, and received still another nod.

Julie recalled, "I now have a beautiful daughter named Elizabeth (but she likes to be called Beth), who will soon be 14. However, throughout the rest of my pregnancy, when I sat in meditation in the circle, I kept hearing the name Gabriel. So much so that if the baby had turned out to be a boy, I would have given him that name. I've since found out that Gabriel is the archangel who transports souls from one life to the next."

Julie was so grateful for Archangel Gabriel's presence, especially after the previous trauma of her son's illness (he is now a healthy 19-year-old). She was able to get through the pregnancy without fear, and her healthy daughter, Elizabeth, was the result. Julie continued to communicate with the angels, including Gabriel, and she is so grateful for all their help.

Divinely Protected Pregnancy

My studies of Archangel Gabriel have been scholarly (reading the Bible and other spiritual texts), and I've conducted field studies of people who've had modern miracles that they credit to Archangel Gabriel's intervention. Some of these miracles have occurred spontaneously, without the person calling specifically for Gabriel. In such cases, I believe that God sends the most appropriate specialist to help with each situation.

Each archangel has a specialty. For instance, Archangel Michael is in charge of ridding the world of evil and fear. Archangel Raphael is the angel of healing, stemming from his restoring sight to the blind man Tobit in the noncanonical Book of Tobit.

Archangel Gabriel's specialty is twofold: functioning as the messenger angel with the copper trumpet and as the angel who announces and helps with conception, pregnancy, birth, and early childhood.

Over the years, I've received hundreds of stories from mothers who asked for Archangel Gabriel's help with their pregnancy, as in the following story from a Russian woman named Elena Sorokina.

When Elena became pregnant with her first child, she also became more sensitive to energies. With this change, she began to feel the presence of angels around her and her child. In her second trimester, Elena found an Archangel Gabriel statue that she'd forgotten she'd purchased years earlier. As Elena gazed at Gabriel's beautiful face on the statue, an inner knowing and recognition told her that this energy was the same protective presence she'd always felt around her.

She heard Gabriel say to her, "Everything's going to be fine with you. You've made everything right. And now I'm going to be your guardian angel."

Since then, Elena has constantly felt Gabriel's calming presence. She says:

> Thanks to Gabriel and Mother Mary, my pregnancy was ideal: My blood pressure was always normal; analyses were wonderful. I had no pains or edemas. I did aqua aerobics and walked as fast as before the pregnancy.
>
> I felt quiet, protected, and strong. It seemed to me I glowed from the inside out. When the time of childbirth came, I asked Archangel Gabriel and Mother Mary to be with me. It was a painful but fast delivery. My son was healthy and calm. We were given a one-person room, although the maternity hospital was overcrowded that night.
>
> Everything *was* really fine, as Archangel Gabriel had said to me. I felt his loving presence and protection, also, the first two years after my son's birth. Thank you, God, Mary, and Archangel Gabriel, for your unconditional love and so much needed help! I wish all expectant and young mothers would accept Gabriel's help into their lives!

I do, too, Elena!

High-Risk Pregnancies

Sometimes pregnancies go awry, with serious conditions that threaten the baby's health. Archangel Gabriel brings about God's healings in miraculous ways.

Amanda Bain was eager to share the story of how her second child, Gabriella, got her name. When Amanda was pregnant, she had a routine 30-week ultrasound. Her obstetrician told her the very upsetting news that her baby had a choroid plexus cyst in her brain and that she needed to have a level II ultrasound. The results showed that there was a large, isolated cyst in her baby's brain, with a 1-in-300 chance that it could cause trisomy 18, a genetic disorder associated with such severe mental dysfunction that the pregnancy would have to be terminated.

Because Amanda was only 23 and had no family history of birth defects, her doctor didn't recommend an amniocentesis. They just had to wait it out and hope that the cyst would dissipate on its own in the third trimester.

Amanda's mother, Lisa, a certified Angel Therapy Practitioner® who had taken my course in 2006, told her daughter to call upon Archangel Gabriel, a protector and nurturer of pregnant women and children.

Amanda told me, "I spoke daily to Archangel Gabriel and vowed that if the cyst in my baby's brain was resolved, I would name her Gabriella in her honor. In a follow-up ultrasound in the third trimester, we could see that the cyst was completely gone. She was born about ten days late, but wide-eyed, alert, and very healthy. She had beautiful copper-colored ringlets, which she still has today at nearly four years old, and big pale blue eyes.

Whenever I draw an Archangel Gabriel card from my *Archangel Oracle Cards* deck, I smile at the likeness between my beautiful daughter and her namesake."

How beautiful that Amanda's daughter has copper hair, the same color as Archangel Gabriel's trumpet!

Giving Birth

Archangel Gabriel continues to hold the hands of expectant mothers throughout their pregnancies, and into their birthing experiences.

Going into labor during a healthy pregnancy is frightening enough! So when medical challenges arise, Archangel Gabriel helps the mother and child stay calm, centered, and healthy.

I can only imagine how terrified Nelly Coneway must have been during her birthing complications,

which were nearly fatal for her *and* her child. Thank God Archangel Gabriel saved both of their lives!

Nothing during Nelly's pregnancy could have prepared her for the complications that would occur when she was giving birth. Her daily exercises and meditations helped her stay active and happy, but then early on the morning of April 29, 1991, she felt the contractions begin. Despite the cold, rainy day and the thick fog covering the city, she felt magic in the air. Something was telling her to expect a miracle.

In the hospital, after hours of pain, there was no sign that Nelly's baby would arrive soon. When the doctors examined her, she read from their faces that something was very wrong, but her pain was so unbearable that she drifted away.

Nelly recalled:

> As if I were in a dream, I heard them saying, "We're losing both of them. The umbilical cord is entangled around the baby's neck. We need to use forceps, now."
>
> The last thing I remember is praying for Mother Mary and the angels to save my baby. Later that day, I clearly saw a beautiful woman dressed in white who woke me up. She hovered above me, and rays of golden light illuminated the room, a contrast to the dark day outside. The love that was coming from her was overwhelming, and I gratefully melted into her copper aura. She smiled at me and said, "Congratulations, you gave birth to a beautiful boy. He is healthy and will bring many blessings to you and to the world."
>
> I just knew that she was an angel, sent by God to assure me that my baby *was* okay. I was

so happy that I would soon meet him. Then I saw a clear vision of Archangel Gabriel, assuring me that my baby would be fine.

Minutes later, a doctor came in and told me that I had a son. Without thinking, I said, "Yes, I know."

She looked at me—stunned—but continued, "Your baby is in an incubator for observation because of complications with his breathing. He needs to stay here for two more weeks. What a lucky boy he is to have survived!"

My son had been born at 11:11 A.M. I prayed again for his continued health. Every day I went to see my son in the incubator and looked at his tiny body, sending him all my love and prayers for perfect health and strength.

This experience reminded Nelly of the story of her own birth. She'd been born two months premature, and no one thought that she'd make it, but she surprised everybody with her passion for life. Her son, too, was learning an important lesson on the Earth plane.

"You are strong; you are healthy," Nelly kept telling him. That and the thought that the loving angel Gabriel was with him, too, helped her have faith that her son would be okay. Every morning and night, Nelly went into the hospital's little chapel, named after St. George, until a miracle happened. A few days later, the doctor told her that her son was doing very well and he could go home. It was the day of St. George: May 6, 1991.

Nelly told me, "Thanks to God and the angels, my son was completely healed and is now a happy, smart, strong young man. I will never forget the beautiful angel

who enfolded me in her wings and gave me hope that all would be fine. Thank you, dear Gabriel!"

What an amazing experience for both Nelly and her son! When you go through a life-threatening trauma, your faith in God can either be increased or it can disappear if you can't see the behind-the-scenes miracles and blessings. Fortunately, Nelly and her son choose to focus upon the beauty within their brush with death. They see their birth miracles as a part of their souls' lessons, which make them stronger and wiser.

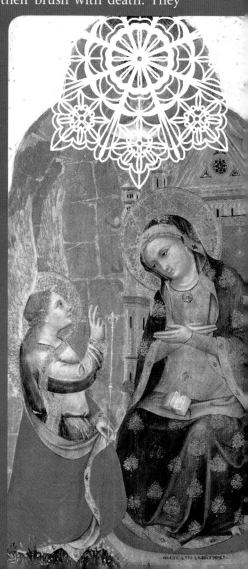

Joanne S. Kuhenbeaker's daughter-in-law also had serious birthing complications that were life threatening. So Joanne called upon God and Archangel Gabriel for protection, and the baby was born healthy!

Joanne's daughter-in-law had gotten pregnant a few years ago but miscarried. She became pregnant again a year later, and because she had a kidney-shaped uterus, she had to have ultrasounds every month. Due to these many tests, Joanne was aware of every little detail that most mothers-in-law wouldn't necessarily know about.

It was quite frightening for Joanne to hear things like "The baby's cord is around its neck," or "The baby is in the wrong position, and if it stays that way, it could die." It made the pregnancy quite frightening for everyone, and Joanne prayed continually for her son and his wife. Joanne recalled:

I was praying one day and happened to look at the footstool in front of me. There was a publication called *Inspirations* that I'd received in the mail. I read an article about angels that told how Archangel Gabriel would protect new mothers and their pregnancies. From that day on, I asked God and Gabriel for the perfect pregnancy, labor, delivery, and baby to be born to my son and his wife.

Well, everything I prayed for happened. When the baby was delivered, the nurse took a photo of the newborn. A second later, she yelled, "There's an angel in the picture!" And there was—it was an angel with yellowish-green wings kissing the baby's face. I know that Archangel Gabriel was with my granddaughter the moment I asked for her help. Gabriel was with her right through the delivery.

From the day she was born, Joanne's granddaughter, who was named Riley, seemed to be an extraordinary baby. Joanne happened to read a book on Crystal Children, and Riley fit the description exactly. She also went to an Angel Therapist, who upon seeing Riley's photograph, remarked, "She's a Crystal Child delivered by an angel." Joanne knows that the angel was Gabriel.

Joanne's story shows that you can call upon Archangel Gabriel on behalf of someone else. As long as that individual is open to receiving heavenly help (angels won't violate someone's freewill choices), Gabriel will go to that person immediately.

❧   ❧

Archangel Gabriel monitors pregnancies and gives clear and unmistakable guidance to mothers, to ensure the health of both mother and child. Emilie Jones received this form of aid from Gabriel during her pregnancy. Because God and the angels respect our free will, they cannot impose guidance upon us. All they can do is offer it to us and pray that we listen and take action, as Emilie did.

When Emilie was pregnant with her third child, she had a powerful visit from Gabriel. She saw and heard the archangel tell her to go to the hospital immediately. The archangel literally said, "Go!"

Emilie listened to the message and immediately went to the hospital, where tests revealed that her unborn baby's heart rate had dropped dangerously low. Her doctor decided upon an emergency C-section to save the baby. Emilie called upon Gabriel for help, and she heard the archangel whisper calmly, "Cast all fears aside. Everything's going to be fine."

The doctor said there was no time for an epidural or spinal shot to take effect, so he had Emilie put under general anesthesia. When she awoke, she had a healthy baby son!

Ten months later, Archangel Gabriel appeared to Emilie again. As she stood in the shower (a place where many people receive inspiration due to the water's spiritual-opening effects), Emilie heard Gabriel's distinctive voice say, "You will be pregnant."

Emilie gasped and protested, "I can't be! I'm on a low dose of progesterone, and I am nursing my baby." Then Emilie realized that she was arguing with an angel, and

she said, "If I am pregnant, I will honor that with love and gratitude. But I will also need help, as I have been taking progesterone and nursing my new baby."

Sure enough, Emilie's home pregnancy test read positive. She'd always wanted four children (and four in angel numbers means "The angels are with you!"). Emilie laughed that heaven is much stronger than any birth control!

Because she'd been on progesterone, Emilie's doctors did blood tests and warned her that she might not be able to carry the baby to term. Emilie prayed daily over her womb, and heard Archangel Gabriel insist that she'd have a full-term, healthy baby without a C-section. And she did!

Today, Emilie and her husband co-parent with the angels. They both consult with Archangel Gabriel in caring for their four beautiful children. And now Emilie is an Angel Therapy Practitioner who helps others connect with Gabriel as well.

People are constantly asking me why some people like Emilie appear to receive God's help, while others seem to be ignored. I really believe that God tries to help everyone, but occasionally people don't hear, believe, or follow the Divine warnings that are given through angels. That's why it's so important to keep a clear and sober mind, as intoxication can prevent you from hearing your angels' guidance.

It's equally important to have faith in God's guidance, even if it seems illogical. You can always ask God and the angels for additional signs and verification, if you're unsure of the validity of the guidance you receive. But in cases such as Emilie's, time is often of the essence.

Thank God she took immediate action when Archangel Gabriel told her to go to the hospital!

Nurses and Angels

Those who deliver babies have lots of interactions with angels! For instance, Lisa Bolton, a labor-and-delivery nurse, has asked Archangel Gabriel to help her with difficult deliveries many times. It seems like the angel always guides nurses and doctors to make the right choices.

Lisa said, "I feel that my prayers are answered every time I ask for help. Most recently, I prayed for a lady who was bleeding so much during delivery that I thought she was going to die. Miraculously, the bleeding stopped for a few minutes, which allowed all the required staff to arrive and get her to the operating room. We were able to stop the bleeding, and she was fine to go home a few days later with her healthy baby. I'm so grateful for Archangel Gabriel's continual help!"

Over the years, I've heard many such stories from nurses and other health-care professionals who pray and call upon angels. If I had to have medical care, I would definitely opt to work with someone who prays—wouldn't you?

✧   ✧

Another nurse, Audrey, told me how working with Archangel Gabriel helped her ob-gyn office attract more patients!

Audrey is a registered nurse, and she was worried because there was a considerable decrease in the overall patient load. The woman who took care of the billing in the office noted that she'd been working there for 15 years and had never seen such a decrease in patients.

Everyone was getting worried about being laid off, as they all had families to support, so each morning on the way to work, Audrey would ask Archangel Gabriel to send new patients to the office and to bless the practice. A few weeks later, a co-worker of Audrey's who took appointments told her that they were booked for the next several weeks. (And a year later, the office was still busy.) Audrey said:

> Since Gabriel helped so much with the patient load, I decided to ask the archangel to help some of our infertile patients. Again, each morning on my way to work, I would thank Gabriel for helping several patients get pregnant. One woman was in her early 40s and had tried various

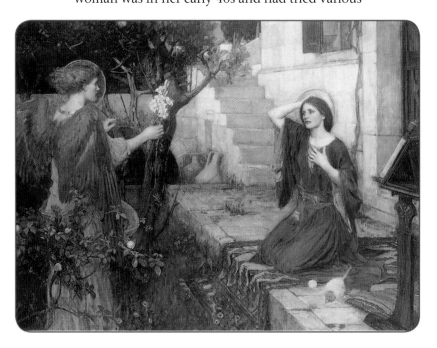

options to treat infertility for years without success. But right before she and her husband completed adoption applications, she found out she was pregnant and ended up having a healthy son.

Another woman had gone through several miscarriages, but then had a healthy daughter. And still another couldn't believe that she'd gotten pregnant without the aid of fertility drugs, which she'd needed in the past. I thank Archangel Gabriel for these miracles!

Healers who work in fields involving conception and pregnancy can follow Audrey's example and ask Archangel Gabriel to assist with clients and patients.

Spiritually Healing Infertility

With rising infertility and sterility rates, Archangel Gabriel can help parents who desperately want a child. I've seen Gabriel help prospective adoptive parents successfully adopt. I've also seen people overcome fertility issues to successfully conceive, by calling upon God and the angels. This includes my own birth!

My parents were married seven years and really wanted a child, but my mother wasn't conceiving. So finally, she put in a prayer request at her local Unity church. I was conceived ten months later! Is it any wonder that I believe in the power of prayer, since I was born with the help of prayers?

Here's the letter my parents received after they put in their prayer request:

Science of Mind Church

DR. FREDERICK BAILES, DIRECTOR

128 SOUTH LA BREA AVENUE
LOS ANGELES 36, CALIFORNIA
WEBSTER 8-4177

September 25, 1956

Mrs. Joan Hannan
608A Mariposa
Burbank, Calif.

Dear Mrs. Hannan:

Thank you for your letter and enclosed check for $5.00. Dr. Bailes wants you to know that he has given treatment for the requests you have made. Also, that he will include it for Sunday's silent meditation period, where the vast audience joins in unified prayer as it turns its consciousness in your direction.

With very best wishes for an ever-increasing manifestation of all the Good in your life and affairs, including your dear ones.

Sincerely,

Robert Cabal

Robert Cabal
Secretary

When my parents tried for seven years to conceive without success, they finally put in a prayer request, and I was conceived within ten months.

In my book *Angel Medicine,* I included the story of a woman named Leisa Machado who successfully overcame infertility with the help of archangels Gabriel and Michael.

I met Leisa at a workshop I gave in the seaside town of Santa Cruz in Northern California. When Leisa asked for an angel reading about the possibility of a pregnancy, I clairvoyantly looked inside of her, which is a process called "medical intuition." I was awestruck (not an exaggeration) by how clean this woman's insides were. All of Leisa's organs looked as sanitary as an operating room. Her chakras were pristine, and she absolutely glowed from the inside. Never before or since have I seen such a clean internal body!

Leisa told me that she ate organic foods exclusively, avoided all chemicals, and drank only distilled water because she felt that all other water had potentially harmful microbes. I was happy to hear this, since GMOs (genetically modified organisms), GE (genetic engineering), and high-tech agriculture have been shown to lead to sterility. Certified-organic foods are the only way to avoid these bioengineered toxins, especially in the U.S. and Canada, where GE is unregulated.

Leisa explained that she and her husband wanted to have a baby, and she thought the best way was to prepare her body as well as possible. Still, she was having difficulty conceiving.

She'd had three tubal pregnancies, a miscarriage, and one failed attempt at in vitro fertilization. After six years of trying to conceive, Leisa worried that she was getting older and was still without a child. That's when she decided to use a holistic approach to child conception. Leisa embarked upon a path of spirituality, which involved praying, eating organic meals, and holding positive thoughts.

She attended my angel workshop shortly after beginning this process. I psychically saw that Leisa would successfully conceive and birth a child; however, it would be at least two years in the future. Leisa didn't like this news—she wanted a child sooner. So I asked the angels for a message, and they said Leisa could perhaps conceive more quickly with the help of archangels Michael and Gabriel. Michael helps clear the energetic body of the effects of fear, which could potentially delay any goal—including the conception of a baby.

Leisa recalled what she did after the workshop:

> I began to meditate and pray on the situation, and felt guided to call upon not only archangels Gabriel and Michael, but also Raphael. Doreen had mentioned that Gabriel was known for helping during pregnancy. Michael had always been there for me in the past, and I called upon Raphael, the healing angel, for help to be physically ready for conception and pregnancy.
>
> I started meditating twice a day, visualizing each angel doing his unique work on my body and spirit to prepare me to conceive. During one of these meditations, my angels told me that my child could come sooner than Divinely planned, as long as I continued to train as a child counselor. The angels urged me to surrender my fears to God, and when I would get frustrated, I'd say to my angels, "I can't take this anymore; you need to do this for me."
>
> Finally, I got my miracle. Although second in vitro attempts are successful only about 20

percent of the time, it worked for me. I was finally pregnant with a healthy embryo! I can only
thank the angels for this, and acknowledge that
it wouldn't have happened had I not remembered to continually ask for support.

Thank God I learned this lesson, too, because I would need angelic help throughout most of my pregnancy. During the first few weeks, I started to bleed. My doctor put me on bed rest, and I put my three special archangels (Gabriel, Michael, and Raphael) to task, calling upon them continually. I could (and still can) feel each one near a certain side of my body, keeping me at peace.

After a few weeks, I was permitted to get up. My second trimester was fine, but at week 31, I began to go into labor. In the hospital, I felt an incredible outpouring of love and healing. The angels told me that this baby was a pure spirit and that he needed me to stay as pure as possible in order to honor his arrival in the world.

I was again reminded to surrender and "let him go." The wording was unusual and quite frightening, however. I was terrified that it meant I would lose him. I relearned that I needed to let go of trying to hold on to him myself. At week 34, I gave birth to Jaren, a strong and healthy baby boy, named for the Hebrew word for "outcry of joy." He was premature, but breathing on his own and very responsive cognitively.

But Jaren wasn't out of the woods yet. About eight hours after he was born, he took a turn for the worse: he stopped breathing and went into a coma. The doctors couldn't figure out what was wrong with him. In her grief and panic, Leisa turned to her angels. She thought, *This can't be happening! They've guided me through every step! I can't lose him now!*

As she sobbed in her hospital bed, Leisa felt a gentle presence that calmed her with warmth and love. Leisa and her husband sent out a call for prayers. They called friends, who in turn called and e-mailed other friends. They soon felt numerous prayers, and an abundance of Reiki energy and angelic assistance, coming in to help them.

Leisa said, "I could actually see Jaren surrounded by layers and layers of angels! At times, I could see his spirit float up with them, but his feet always stayed grounded in his body. Two days later, doctors were amazed by his miraculous recovery. And just a week and a half later, my husband and I took our little miracle home with us, where he belongs."

Leisa's story reminds us of the importance of talking to God and our angels continually, and then adhering to the Divine guidance that they give us. An important part of Leisa's journey was her willingness to let go. This wasn't always easy for her. Often Leisa had to ask the angels to help her, since the goal of pregnancy was so dear to her heart.

Her story illustrates the principle of surrender. Even though Leisa had a crystal clear desire to have a baby, she was also willing to have the faith necessary to surrender this desire and trust in Divine order completely. I've since heard from Leisa over the years, and she and Jaren are doing very well!

⚞ ⚞

After childbirth, Archangel Gabriel continues to support children and their families, as you'll read about in the next chapter.

⚞ ⚞ ⚞

Chapter Two

PARENTING
AND CHILDHOOD

Archangel Gabriel doesn't just help parents with conception, pregnancy, and birth—the angel nurtures children, and co-parents through every aspect of their young lives. Over the years, I've talked with countless moms and dads who called upon Gabriel for guidance with resolving sibling rivalries, confronting developmental issues, eating and nutrition, child care, schooling, confusion about vaccines and other medications, and so forth.

It's said that parents' prayers for their children are answered first in heaven. In fact, God, Jesus, Mother Mary, and Archangel Gabriel can and will do *anything* to ensure your family's health and well-being. All it takes on your part is asking for help, and then carefully listening to the guidance you receive in the form of feelings, intuition, inspired ideas, and signs.

As with all angels, Gabriel follows God's will for us. The archangels know how to assist us in ways that exceed our expectations. That's why it's important to ask for help without specifying how we want that help to occur, as God's solution will be creative, peaceful, harmonious, and a win-win for everyone involved. If we impose our own agenda upon how our prayers are to be answered, then we may miss an angel pointing us in a better direction.

Sweet Dreams

"Night-night" time is anything but an occasion for rest in many households where children suffer from insomnia, night terrors, and sleep disorders. Researchers estimate that 30 to 40 percent of children don't get enough sleep, and have found that childhood insomnia is correlated with learning and behavioral disorders.

When children can't sleep, that usually means a sleepless night for harried parents as well. Fortunately, you can call upon Archangel Gabriel to help with all aspects of childhood health, including guaranteeing a good night's sleep, as a woman named Angela Tyack discovered. Angela told me:

> I developed a close relationship with Archangel Gabriel after my baby was waking up an average of seven times a night. I remember one particular night begging Archangel Gabriel for help, comfort, and sleep for my son. That night,

Nate slept for eight hours straight! Since then, he only wakes up twice a night.

Before I go to sleep, I ask Archangel Gabriel to stay with us and continue to encourage Nate to sleep soundly and peacefully. I thank God and Archangel Gabriel for the blessings, love, and support.

Archangel Gabriel is a nurturing angel who ensures peace in children's minds and bodies. Sensitive adults can feel and hear the presence of Gabriel, and some—like a mother named Lorna*—can also *see* the archangel.

Lorna is a 33-year-old full-time mother to her three children. One evening, she carried her two-year-old daughter, Sarah*, into her bedroom for a feeding. The lights were off, but Lorna saw a shadow silhouette of angel wings on the wall right next to her bed. She was surprised but felt happy and safe. She sat on the bed to feed Sarah and then noticed a deep orange color around her daughter. Lorna felt deeply peaceful, and she relaxed even more.

---

* Lorna asked that her and her daughter's names be changed for this book, because she is aware that her story sounds so unusual that others may doubt it. But *she* knows that she really saw the wings and orange glow and that she heard the archangel's name. (Throughout the book, I've marked names that have been changed at the request of the storyteller with an asterisk.)

That's when Lorna heard a voice say to her that Sarah was a very special and sensitive little girl, and that the angel who was speaking would help guide Lorna in teaching her daughter.

The experience seemed natural and wonderful to Lorna. When she asked for the angel's name, she heard: "Gabriel, Gabriel." Lorna sat stunned for a few moments and noticed the orange light gently glowing over Sarah's face.

Later, Lorna read my book *Archangels 101* and was amazed to find out that Gabriel's energy color is copper (which is very similar to the orange hue she'd witnessed), and that Gabriel helps with parenting. Lorna says, "I feel that my children and I are truly blessed, and I look forward to continuing to work with the angels to nurture my children, and in all aspects of our lives."

God's Infinite Supply

Parenting isn't an easy role, although it's filled with wonderful rewards. When finances are tight, though, raising a family can be even more stressful. No matter what the world's economic picture, God and the angels will help see to it that your family's needs are met.

This touching story from a 21-year-old man named Crystal Sven Kabongo of Brussels, Belgium, shows the manifestation power of Archangel Gabriel.

Crystal's mother's name is Gabrielle, and she grew up with the ability to see and talk to angels and Mother Mary. She taught this ability to her young son.

When Crystal was a high school senior, his teacher announced a two-week trip to the beautiful country of Senegal. All the students were happy to go, but Crystal worried whether his mother could afford to send him on the trip.

When he asked his mother whether he could go to Senegal with his classmates, she replied that there wasn't enough money in her bank account, but somehow they would pay for the trip. She told Crystal, "I'll just ask my archangel, Archangel Gabriel, who I know will help me have this money. Don't worry, and have faith. You will go to Senegal."

Crystal asked how the angel would do this. His mother replied, "Just have faith. Archangel Gabriel is really powerful. Don't be afraid . . . have faith."

Crystal wondered how his mother could be so certain that she'd receive such a large amount of money. Sure enough, though, two months later an unexpected check arrived! It was money owed to Crystal's mother that she'd completely forgotten about.

Crystal says, "I know that Archangel Gabriel has always had this subtle connection with my mom and helps her every day. That is why I love to learn about angels and archangels."

Just as Jesus taught us about the power of faith, so did Crystal's mother demonstrate that unwavering faith brings miracles. Of course, when you're afraid, it's not always easy to stay peacefully centered like Crystal's mother. Stress quickens your breathing rate, blocks your creative insights, and darkens your moods and outlook. That's where the angels can bring light back into your life, if you'll ask for their help.

For example, Cherilyn Schlange was worried about her finances, and wondered how she'd pay her bills and have enough money to feed her children and herself. She began repeating the names of three archangels in her mind: "Gabriel, Michael, Raphael."

Immediately, Cherilyn heard a soft male voice in her right ear say, "Stop worrying, Cheri. It's going to be okay. Don't worry."

Right away, Cherilyn felt calm, and she slept well that night. She says, "I woke up to a glorious day, and in the end, everything was okay and turned out wonderfully well."

Of course it did! Life will always take a turn for the better, although it may not seem that way at the time. When we ask for Divine intervention, it's like calling a support team to help shoulder burdens and enact solutions.

Worry never helps anything, but prayer always helps everything.

ᕙ ᕙ ᕙ

Chapter Three

VISIONS OF GABRIEL

Thousands of years after the prophet Daniel, Zechariah, and Mother Mary saw Gabriel, modern people are still encountering this powerful messenger angel. I've talked to people worldwide who've had visions and dreams of Gabriel. Some of them saw Gabriel spontaneously, and others encountered the angel after prayer for help.

Those who've shared these deeply personal stories aren't seeking attention or other worldly gratification. They're instead left awestruck by the experience, and feeling deeply grateful to God. Many are humbled and wonder, *Why would Archangel Gabriel visit me?*

When we remember that the angels are unlimited beings who can be with everyone simultaneously, it's not so odd that "ordinary folks" would receive visitations. After all, to God, we are *all* extraordinary!

In this chapter, we'll explore the experiences of those whose lives were miraculously changed by their physical and dream encounters with Archangel Gabriel.

Physical Encounters with Angels

"Be not forgetful to entertain strangers: for thereby some have entertained angels unawares."

These words from the New Testament's Epistle to the Hebrews have echoed through my mind because in

recent years, I've talked to increasing numbers of people who have had physical encounters with angels who are in human form. Many of these stories are published in my weekly column in *Woman's World* magazine.

The encounters usually involve people who are in danger, extremely worried about something, or feeling stuck in their lives. Then a stranger appears suddenly who looks like a human man or woman, except for his or her unusual attire (in either formal or tattered clothing) and otherworldly eyes. These figures don't have wings or halos, yet they *are* God's pure angels in human form.

Such a stranger knows personal details, like the person's name or the source of his or her distress, and offers

comforting words, like "Don't worry; it's all going to be fine and work out perfectly well." Or he or she may lend physical help—for example, pulling a stuck car out of the snow with superhuman strength.

Sometimes, the stranger gives a business card or a contact number . . . and later, it's discovered that no such address or phone number exists. Or, if the helpful stranger has an emergency vehicle (incarnated angels sometimes arrive with a tow truck, ambulance, bus, or other vehicle), there is no record of that employee with the service company.

Each of these stories ends in the same way: the helpful stranger always disappears mysteriously, along with the vehicle. In a high percentage of these stories that I receive, the helpful stranger identifies himself as "Michael."

The people relaying these accounts to me have no hidden agendas that I can find. They're not trying to convince or convert anyone, and they don't profit from the story or have a product to sell connected with it. They simply tell the story and say that they know it's true: they met an angel and were miraculously helped by that encounter.

Interestingly, the original story of Archangel Raphael appeared in the noncanonical Book of Tobit, which tells of a helpful stranger who later revealed that he was Raphael. It's rare, though, for me to meet people who've had physical encounters with Archangel Gabriel or any of the other archangels appearing in human form, as in this story recounted by a woman named Roxanne Veillet.

At the age of 16, Roxanne went for a stroll that changed her life. Her teenage years had been spent living by a river, where she would often walk to get much-needed solitude. One day she was particularly drawn to go there. The feeling was so strong that she couldn't deny it.

During this time, Roxanne had been feeling a lot of despair and loneliness. She had just been ridiculed by her family for wanting to pursue a career as a writer, and

she was taking their lack of approval very hard, as she couldn't see herself doing anything else. As far as her family was concerned, writers starved and weren't able to pay their bills.

So Roxanne went down to the river around sunset and sat there for quite some time, until her reverie was broken by a man who appeared beside her. He said he was a photographer, writer, and painter, and asked if he could take her picture as she faced the sunset. He also mentioned that he lived comfortably off of his art.

Roxanne felt healed by his words, which were exactly what she needed to hear at that time. She told him about her worries as if they'd been friends for years, and she found him to be gentle, beautiful, and soothing. Rox-

anne knew instinctively that she could trust him. They talked about creativity and the arts until the sun went down. He then suggested that he walk her home because her parents might be worried.

As they reached her street, the man looked at Roxanne very seriously and said, "My name is Gabriel. Should you ever need to, do not hesitate to call me. I am always available to listen, whatever the time." He was very insistent about that.

Roxanne recalled:

> I asked for his number and added it to the contacts on my cell phone. We said our good-byes, and he walked on. When I turned around

to look at him one last time, he had disappeared. I thought that was odd, but continued on until I reached my house, which was about five minutes away. When I walked inside, I realized that my cell phone had disappeared, too!

I felt completely different after that moment, and knew that something special had happened. As a result, I began exploring my spirituality and my creativity. I am now 23 years old and feel blessed to have discovered God and the angels at such a young age. I work very closely with Gabriel to this day, and I've had numerous signs that he is never too far away.

How very like Archangel Gabriel to help a fledgling artist! As the angel of communication, Gabriel gives encouragement to writers and other human messengers, as you'll read in the next chapter. You'll notice that Roxanne reported feeling safe and comfortable in Gabriel's presence, and this is another telltale sign of a true angelic encounter.

In Roxanne's case, Gabriel appeared in human form because she was too upset to clearly hear Divine reassurance. People who are distressed or anxious often have difficulty receiving heaven's messages or feeling God's presence. When we're upset, our muscles tighten, and our breathing becomes shallow, making us less receptive to feeling, hearing, and seeing the heavenly encouragement that is always available to everyone. That's why God often sends temporarily incarnated angels to clearly and loudly deliver Divine messages.

Dream Encounters with Gabriel

It's not unusual to dream of an angel, and many such dreams are true encounters instead of products of the unconscious mind. Dr. Ian Stevenson of the University of Virginia cataloged thousands of cases of "dream visitations" in which people interacted with their deceased loved ones or angels while asleep. Dr. Stevenson said that the "degree of vividness" is the characteristic that distinguishes true visitations from mere dreams. Visitations include rich colors, intense emotions, and a more-than-real feeling. When you wake from one, the experience stays with you longer than an ordinary dream. You may remember explicit details about it many years after it occurs.

One of the easiest ways to receive Divine guidance (especially if you're feeling stressed or blocked) is to ask for help as you're falling asleep. You can do so aloud, through silent prayer, or even by writing this request on a paper that you place beneath your pillow.

When we're sleeping, our skeptical ego-mind also sleeps, rendering the higher self more open to direct contact with the Divine.

For example, a woman named Elena Covarrubias receives messages and guidance from Archangel Gabriel in her dreams. To Elena, Gabriel appears as a young, thin, dark-skinned male angel.

One time, she dreamed she was in her house with Gabriel, who asked her to follow the angel to the kitchen, where her grandmother sat looking extremely sad. Gabriel asked Elena to give her grandmother a reassuring hug.

The next day during breakfast, Elena noticed that her grandmother indeed seemed very sad. So just like Gabriel had shown her in the previous night's dream, she walked up to her grandma and embraced her. Elena says that after the dream, she expresses love to her grandmother much more often, and they are growing closer as a result.

Dream encounters with angels, particularly with the messenger Archangel Gabriel, give us important guidance such as the kind Elena received, which led to an improved relationship with her grandmother. You can ask to receive Divine messages while you're asleep. You may not remember the dream exactly when you awaken, but heaven's answers will be guiding you from your unconscious.

Over the years, I've received many stories from people who received answers from other people's dreams. If we're too stressed to notice messages, the angels will often take another route through someone else. In the following poignant story, the message was both for the man who had the dream and for his daughter, Susan*.

Recently, Susan passed away after a long illness. She had been doing okay, so no one had expected her to die, at least not for a while. Susan's father dreamed a few days before her passing that Archangel Gabriel came to him, and said that he was taking his daughter to the other side. The father didn't believe in angels, but within a few days of the dream, his daughter took a turn for the worse and did pass away. The doctor on duty at the hospital was named—you guessed it—Dr. Gabriel!

Gabriel was trying to soften the blow of Susan's passing by giving her father advance warning. Sometimes the angels tell us of events not in order for us to prevent them, but rather for us to emotionally prepare for them. And the doctor named for the angel was a heavenly sign that Susan was now with the angels, including Archangel Gabriel.

Angelic Encounters and Near-Death Experiences

What happens to a person's soul after death? Researchers have gathered a lot of information from people who've had "near-death experiences" (NDEs), in which they were clinically dead but were later revived. The NDE phenomenon has been studied by scientists, including those who have had such an experience themselves. Some skeptics believe that the visions reported by NDE'ers are a product of a dying brain deprived of oxygen. Yet there's ample evidence to show that these experiences exceed mere hallucinations. For example, countless NDE'ers can recall what their doctors said after the time when they were considered dead. And other NDE'ers have reported that their souls "flew" around the surgical room or hospital after death and saw items that were later verified (a gym shoe on the hospital roof, for example).

What the NDE'ers report is that when a person crosses over, he or she is met by angels, religious figures (such as Jesus), and departed loved ones (including pets). These beings help the newly crossed-over person assimilate into a new "life" in the spiritual world without a physical body.

For example, Mary Ann Kipuros's mother had a heart attack following her surgery in a hospital. During her recovery she talked about going down a long tunnel into bright lights, where she saw her deceased husband and dog waiting for her. Then Archangel Gabriel met her. She said that she wasn't ready to leave her daughter and Earth life yet. So Gabriel allowed her to return for another few years.

Mary Ann didn't believe her mother's story, nor did she believe in the angels. But then a few years after her mother finally did pass away, something remarkable happened.

Mary Ann received a puppy as a gift, but the dog wouldn't come to her or cooperate. In her mind, Mary Ann could hear her mother's voice saying, "Gabriel, Gabriel." This went on for hours.

Mary Ann realized that her mother was talking to her from heaven and advising that she name the puppy Gabriel. So she tried calling the dog by that name, and the puppy immediately ran into her arms!

Mary Ann said, "Now I tell my friends that my mom named Gabriel from heaven." And *now* she believes.

Tall Gabriel

Many people who have visions of Archangel Gabriel report the angel being extremely tall. Most archangels are taller and stronger than guardian angels. It's sometimes said that the height of an archangel extends from Earth into heaven.

A young woman named Donna had a clear vision of Gabriel as a nearly 90-foot-tall angel. To put that height into perspective, 90 feet would be the same as an eight- or nine-story building, like one that might house a smaller hotel, for example. That's *tall,* I think you'd agree!

Donna's encounter with the tall Gabriel occurred on her birthday when she was severely depressed. As she stood at work that day, she thought of how easily she could end her life and no one would notice or care. She'd just had a big fight with her best friend, who had turned all of her other friends against her.

With nowhere to turn, Donna surrendered her cares completely to God. She recalled:

It was the moment in that void—the moment as quick and as tiny as the point of a needle—that the magic happened. The moment after "giving up" and before the decision to "end it" was when everything changed.

Almost frozen, with all the hair on my body standing on end, I looked up and saw an energy of immense proportions that left my mouth and eyes wide open as I kept scanning upward. It was an archangel looking right at me, and I stared in disbelief. I knew it was Gabriel who had come for me. I was staring at an angel so big that it had to have been almost 90 feet tall, and I was awestruck by its beauty.

I saw such beauty and love. I stared until my insides were calm; I have no idea how much time passed before I felt the need to go back to the work I was doing. I was really weeping now, so I turned away from the other workers who passed by me.

Gabriel had gotten my attention so quickly and had given me so much unconditional love that I needed at that time. I hadn't asked for help that I was aware of. Instead, I had completely surrendered. I was calm enough now to make new plans.

At the time, I had no idea what was going on, and of course I did my research. I discovered that archangels do become as large as the space they're in, and they do show up when you

need them the most. I am in awe of archangels, and I'm humbled by how close I was to ending my life. This taught me to of course ask for help *before* I'm on the verge of letting go of the last thread of hope, and to trust that they are there *all* the time.

Like other people who've had encounters with Archangel Gabriel, Donna found that her life was profoundly changed.

Angels have no physical bodies, so they can appear in whichever way brings us the most comfort. Perhaps Archangel Gabriel appears tall to instill in us a sense of security and protection, much like small children protected by a larger, loving adult.

In this next story, another person saw a giant image of Archangel Gabriel.

Kevin was raised Catholic and always felt a connection to Mother Mary and Archangel Gabriel. He knew that Gabriel's name meant "power and strength of God." One afternoon, Kevin asked Archangel Gabriel for the gift of courage, strength, and power.

That night, Kevin attended a charismatic seminar at his Catholic church. A young man and woman invoked the Holy Spirit as they were laying their hands on Kevin. The young lady had a vision of Archangel Gabriel behind him, standing about 50 feet tall. The young man then told Kevin that he'd received the gift of strength, and that Archangel Gabriel's message to him was: *Your prayers are not in vain.*

Kevin said, "Only later did I remember my prayer to Archangel Gabriel that I'd made earlier that day. I was

so amazed and grateful that my one prayer to Archangel Gabriel for the gift of strength was answered."

Gabriel, like God, Jesus, and all the angels, always responds to prayers. We may not feel or see evidence of this heavenly presence, especially if we're under stress. But the angels are there nonetheless.

Gabriel's Comforting and Healing Presence

God's angels are purely compassionate, and they bring us comfort during our most trying times. They know how difficult earthly life can be. While they may not be able to fix painful situations, they can ease *our* pain, as a woman named Jennifer L. Petrus discovered.

In 2010, Jennifer's beautiful cat, Powder, got very sick. After two weeks of trying desperately to nurse her back to health, Jennifer had to do the hardest thing she'd ever done in her whole life. She had to take Powder to the animal hospital and have her put down.

Jennifer couldn't leave Powder's side the entire time. She told me, "I'm in tears as I write this to you. She was the most precious little girl anyone could ask to have grace her life. I stayed with her, and she just steadily looked into my eyes with such trust. I could hear her telling me that she had to go and that she loved me. It was very peaceful—but nonetheless difficult, even though it was the most humane thing I could have done. I cried for days, even while I was at work decorating cakes."

After Jennifer got off work on Thanksgiving morning, she came home to take a nap and cried herself to sleep. While she was napping, she had a vivid encounter that was much more than a dream: Archangel Gabriel

came to her while she rested, and it was the most real thing that she'd ever experienced with her eyes shut. Jennifer recalled:

> Archangel Gabriel stood at the foot of my bed. In shock I froze, and then grabbed for my husband's arm, but he was no longer lying next to me. Archangel Gabriel was then above me.
>
> I could feel all of the pain being pulled out of me. I jumped up from the bed, hearing my husband in the kitchen. I ran for him and grabbed him, pointing toward the hallway where Gabriel stood. And next to the angel was a beautiful orb

of light, just beaming to every end of the room. I heard Powder meow, and then they were gone. I woke from my nap filled with peace.

Two weeks later, Jennifer went to the rescue organization Angels for Animals and brought home a little golden kitten whom she lovingly called Gabriel. She and her husband care for him very much and know that he could never replace their sweet Powder, but they're grateful that they can share their love with their new "son."

Archangel Gabriel is both strong and sensitive, enabling whoever is in the angel's presence to feel calm and protected, as Jennifer described.

Gabriel's Copper Trumpet

Because Gabriel's symbolic horn is copper, people often report seeing flashes of copper or orange lights in the angel's presence. Seeing colored lights is quite normal among those who've encountered an archangel or ascended master. Over the years, I've found that people who have had a vision or dream visit report the following colors glowing around the being, or in physically visible flashes of light:

- **Jesus Christ:** Gold
- **Mother Mary:** Pale blue
- **Archangel Michael:** Royal blue
- **Archangel Raphael:** Emerald green
- **Archangel Gabriel:** Copper or orange

A friend of mine, Carmen Carignan, even captured Archangel Gabriel's colors in a photo!

A few years ago, Carmen (a registered nurse who practices alternative medicine) decided to fulfill the dream of creating her own space for her private healing practice. It was a huge step for her, as she knew she'd be coming out of the closet, so to speak. Finding a place was overwhelming, as was the notion of having the means to pay the monthly rent. She could have chosen to keep procrastinating, but she could feel the nudging inside of her. Not wanting to do this work alone, she called upon Gabriel, as she knew that this archangel helps people with changes, communication, and putting things into place. Carmen's nursing specialty has been birthing, and she's had many miraculous experiences with calling upon Archangel Gabriel to help mothers and babies.

After Carmen called upon Archangel Gabriel's help in finding a location for her healing practice, two amazing things happened:

- First, within a few days, she captured an angelic presence in a photo one evening when she was attempting to take a picture of the full moon. The angel had a coppery aura, with the most beautiful large wings.

- She found an orange feather that filled her with total confidence that all would be well.

She knew Archangel Gabriel was responsible because of the love and the immediate sense of comfort that entered her being when she saw the photo and found the feather.

Carmen recalled: "The next morning, a therapist friend of mine called to ask me if I was still looking for a place to rent. When I said yes, she told me that another therapist was leaving town and wanted to make sure someone doing healing work would rent her room. I decided to check it out. It was in the perfect location, and less expensive than what I'd thought I would have to pay. It also had the added perk of beautiful trees outside the windows. My therapist friend helped me get situated, answered

numerous questions, and even helped me get a sign permit. She was an angel sent to me by an angel!"

Carmen strongly believes that Archangel Gabriel led her to find the ideal site for her healing practice, which is still thriving many years later. She says, "I give thanks to Archangel Gabriel, who helped me find the perfect place, and at the perfect location and price. The transition into this new healing space went very smoothly thanks to this wonderful angel."

Archangel Gabriel offers us comfort while lending us strength and courage. In the next chapter, we'll look at how Gabriel helps human messengers: writers!

Chapter Four

GABRIEL'S WRITERS

All angels are messengers of God, each with an individual specialty. Yet, we most often think of Archangel Gabriel as *the* messenger among the messengers. After all, Gabriel's famous announcements to Daniel (the prophet), Zechariah, and the Blessed Mother were world changing.

Gabriel's messages continue to resound through the world. The archangel also delivers important information through people, particularly writers.

In Catholicism, Archangel Gabriel is the patron saint of those who work in communication careers, such as journalists and writers, and messengers such as letter carriers. But you don't need to be Catholic or even religious to receive this angel's assistance with your messenger work, because Gabriel is a nondenominational angel who helps all Earth Angel messengers.

As a reminder, we don't pray to angels, as we aren't deifying them or making them into idols. However, we can ask God to send Gabriel's help or call upon the archangel directly. For example, you can say:

"Dear Archangel Gabriel, thank you for giving me the courage, focus, and motivation to write. Thank you for helping me hear true Divine messages that I can express through the written word."

In this chapter, you'll read many stories of would-be writers and published authors whose work was elevated to new heights on the wings of Archangel Gabriel.

Lisa, a reader of my books, wrote the following to me:

I wasn't convinced that I was supposed to be a writer, although it had been one of my goals since childhood. I'd get excited creating children's books with pictures. Anytime I was asked what I wanted to do with my life, I'd answer, "I want to be a writer."

I remember people replying, "Really? That's a tough thing to be." As I got older, I started to believe these remarks, and became unsure about writing as a career.

I tried writing and submitting magazine articles, but always got rejection letters. I knew other authors in my shoes had dealt with this, too, including you [Doreen], but I kept putting myself below their stature and not realizing they had to work to be published as well. I kept forgetting this, and logically came up with: *That's how awful I am. Look at how quickly they found success and got published, and I can't do that.*

But anytime I pulled cards concerning my career path from the *Archangel Oracle Cards* deck, I got the "Creative Writing" card featuring Archangel Gabriel. And with the *Life Purpose Oracle Cards,* the "Writing" and "Travel" cards appeared anytime I asked for career advice.

Still, I'd given up on my writing dream and would decide, *No, this can't be for me.* This belief was reinforced with each rejection slip I received.

I really wanted to write from home, and knew there had to be something in store for me. I called upon Gabriel many times to help me get my work out there and get me writing gigs that paid and would be published.

My dear friend who is an Angel Therapy Practitioner told me Archangel Gabriel was one of the main angels with me, and to keep writing because it was going to work out.

And it did! I am now paid to write a monthly column about angels for an online spiritual magazine! I know it's thanks to Gabriel and also the help she sent. I now realize that the delay in my writing career was Gabriel's way of giving me the opportunity to practice and polish my writing skills. I am going to keep calling upon Gabriel, as I have lots of other writing and creative projects to get out in the world. Archangel Gabriel: thanks again!

Since 1995, when I began interviewing people about their angel experiences, I've heard and received many stories similar to Lisa's. Gabriel gives motivation, courage, and opportunities to those who feel guided to write.

I believe that the *desire* to write is a signal that it's part of your life purpose. Those who continually think, *I should write,* are getting Divine guidance to express heavenly messages through a book, article, blog, or other medium. In some cases, Gabriel will suggest journaling or keeping a diary as a way of opening the creative pipelines. Whatever form the writing takes, the process of putting pen to paper or fingers to keyboard is soul-stirring.

As this next story illustrates, Gabriel can also help you change the genre of writing you engage in.

Kevin Hunter has worked as a writer in the film business since 1996. He knew that he'd eventually write his own books, because of his passion for writing. Kevin feels that it is his calling and life purpose.

So he began calling upon Archangel Gabriel to help with his writing career, and has come to do so daily. As a result, ideas for writing pour into him, and he's enthusiastic and motivated to write. He even polished and rewrote three old stories that had sat dormant for years.

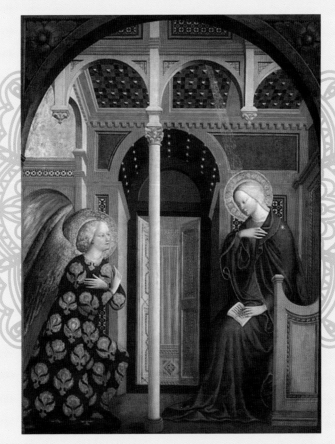

Since calling upon Archangel Gabriel, Kevin has written, edited, and published three books, with more on the way. He says:

> The ideas are overflowing in me and haven't stopped. My writing continues to improve, and I owe it to Archangel Gabriel for being my own personal author's agent.
> I also call upon Archangel Uriel to infuse me with ideas and highlight the next step. When

I write a scene for my book, Gabriel and Uriel show me the next scene, and so forth. It's like the old Michael Jackson video "Billie Jean," where he's dancing outside on the street and each of the steps lights up in front of him as he moves.

Kevin is correct in that Archangel Gabriel does function like a modern-day literary agent, who motivates writers to complete their books and articles and make their deadlines. I've heard stories of Gabriel urging writers to stay awake late at night in order to finish their manuscripts. For this reason, I've often referred to Gabriel respectfully as a "nudging angel." I've even "warned" would-be writers that if they call upon Gabriel for help, they won't be getting much sleep until their manuscript is complete!

Such was the case with a young woman named Jessyka Wallace.

From a very young age, Jessyka has enjoyed writing. During her teen years, she spent all her free time writing stories, poems, and songs. She recalled, "If I had even a minute of free time, I'd pull out my notebook and write!"

She shared these writings with her closest friends and trusted English teachers, and received positive feedback from everyone! One of her teachers even told Jessyka that she should pursue a writing career, which was her dream. However, once Jessyka entered high school, she heard how hard it was to have a rewarding writing career and how little money writers made. Slowly, her dream faded.

In college, Jessyka majored in criminal justice. While she found the topic interesting, something was missing. She didn't feel as passionate as she thought she should.

Jessyka's best grades always showed up in the form of essays. She was a girl who cringed at multiple-choice exams and shined in 15-page papers.

College was a struggle until her junior year when she began on her spiritual path. Jessyka learned how we are designed to follow our passions and are best serving God when we are doing so. She learned how talents are no accident; we are given them for a reason. She also learned about the angels and how we can ask them for help and guidance. Shortly thereafter, Jessyka made the scariest decision of her life and withdrew from college.

She felt terrified and liberated at the same time. It was her first time doing something completely for herself. Even so, she didn't know where to go from there. Each time she'd ask God or the angels what she should be doing, the answer was always: "Write."

Every time Jessyka sat down to write, she experienced writer's block. For weeks after withdrawing from school, she wrote nothing. All she did was complain about having no ideas and not knowing where to begin.

Then one night at a friend's house, Jessyka flipped through my *Archangels & Ascended Masters* book and came across Archangel Gabriel. Jessyka was already aware of this archangel, but didn't know about the details. Upon reading what I'd written, she realized she needed to work closely with Archangel Gabriel!

She wrote down the invocation:

"Archangel Gabriel, I ask for your presence as I [describe the project]. Please open my creative channels so that I may be truly inspired. Help me open my mind so that I may give birth to unique ideas. And please help me to sustain the energy and motivation to follow through on this inspiration. Thank you, Gabriel."

When she got home, Jessyka repeated these words and had silent conversations with Gabriel. She then snuggled in bed with her notebook and began writing.

It was the first time in years she felt inspired to put pen to paper. Jessyka couldn't write fast enough and had to switch to a laptop because her thoughts were coming so fast. Even while typing, Jessyka struggled to keep up!

Writing Careers

The archangels can help you create a fulfilling career around your life purpose. Archangel Michael knows the contents of the Book of Life (also known as Akashic Records or your Soul's Contract). Your true passion—what you're really interested in doing—is the basis of your Divine life purpose, and Michael can help you discover that purpose and put it into practice. Michael will give you strength, courage, and ideas.

Archangel Raphael helps those who have a life purpose involving healing. He can guide you to the proper schooling, books, and other information you'll need for your healing career.

For those whose life purpose involves writing, Archangel Gabriel opens doors of opportunity, as these next
stories illustrate.

A woman named Shanaya credits Archangel Gabriel for her successful work as an editor and writer. It

began in childhood when Shanaya's mother bought her a glow-in-the-dark sticker of an angel with a trumpet. (As you'll recall, that's the symbol of Gabriel.) Years later, Shanaya's aunt bought her a Gabriel necklace pendant, which was identical to her childhood angel sticker.

Shanaya talked to Gabriel constantly, including about her dream of being a writer. She'd find signs from the archangel in the form of angel stickers on floors. These stickers had no logical origin, and Shanaya knew they were signs from above.

When Shanaya was invited for an interview for a desirable editorial job, she carefully prepared her résumé and writing samples. But when she reached the interview location, she realized that she'd left her paperwork at home! She sat in the reception area, waiting for her interview while imploring Gabriel for help.

Shanaya was amazed when she was brought back to the editor's office, and the editor was holding Shanaya's résumé and writing samples! She realized that she'd sent those papers to the organization prior to the interview.

When she heard the editor say, "We would like to offer you the position of editorial assistant," she knew that Archangel Gabriel had helped her. After that day, Shanaya stopped finding angel stickers on the floor. She didn't need to, as her prayers had been answered!

Shanaya discovered that Archangel Gabriel has the ability to help writers in very practical ways. The angel knows that it's not enough to write an inspirational article or book. There needs to be an outlet for publishing the material.

When I first decided to be a writer, my university teacher tried to discourage me. He said that I'd never be published, so why even try? Thank goodness I didn't listen to him!

As a woman named Janhavi Patel discovered, Archangel Gabriel can help writers beat the odds so that they can make a living with their writing work. Although Janhavi's family was skeptical about her ability to support herself financially as a writer, Archangel Gabriel has championed Janhavi's writing all the way.

Janhavi credits Archangel Gabriel with supporting her flourishing career as an entertainment writer. Her connection to the archangel began consciously when she was chosen to play the part of Archangel Gabriel in her grade-school production of the Christmas story.

Whenever Janhavi calls upon Gabriel, the archangel sends her clear acknowledgments such as Janhavi hearing or seeing the name Gabriel (with her physical senses), or seeing videos or cards related to the archangel.

Janhavi's first writing job was as a movie reviewer, which she enjoyed, but she was concerned about how to keep her opinions objective and also how to shield herself from harsh movies. She immediately watched her writing improve and become more detached so that she could write unbiased movie reviews.

Janhavi says, "If you want help and encouragement with writing, please call upon Gabriel. Everybody can write with the help of this archangel. I knew I wanted to make a career out of writing, yet everybody I knew was against it and wanted me to pursue more conventional degrees. However, I had faith that things would work out for me. I can very happily say that I have had a successful career in entertainment media that has been rewarding in many ways, and now I am ready to do something (mostly through writing) that makes a positive difference in the world!"

≈ ≈

The number of writers I've met who have attributed their success to Archangel Gabriel probably equals the number of people I've met who credit Archangel Michael with saving their lives. Writers are clearly Archangel Gabriel's domain and specialty. That includes (but is not limited to) those with adjunct writing careers, such as editors, publishers, bookstore owners and employees, librarians, and newspaper and media employees. Remember that Gabriel is the patron for everyone in communication careers.

If a writing career is your dream, please don't let anyone dissuade you from pursuing it. Keep writing, and continue to call upon Archangel Gabriel for support.

For a long time, a woman named Bindiya had secretly harbored the dream of writing—of expressing herself through words. But in her family, any sort of creative expression was looked down upon. Life was considered a hardship, so the primary focus was on making money and meeting material needs. Bindiya was basically

brought up in an environment that believed in lack, so when she left a high-paying job to explore her creative potential and spirituality, she didn't receive much support from anyone except her brother. One good thing was that no one stopped her or created any obstacles for her—they just ignored her, probably thinking that she would come to her senses soon enough.

Leaving the job was a difficult decision for Bindiya, but she knew that she had to explore her inner potential. After three years of rigorous energy-clearing processes fueled by meditation and various self-growth programs, she took an online course on angels, and was subsequently introduced to my *Archangel Oracle Cards* deck. She was struggling with finances and couldn't afford to purchase the cards, but they found their way to her as a surprise gift from her very supportive brother. Bindiya recalled:

At about the same time, I was looking for a writer's job, but wherever I applied, a portfolio was mandatory and I had none. I saw a newspaper ad for a magazine looking for freelance writers and decided to give it a try even though I'd only started to come out of my creative shell and had no confidence. But I had begun picking a daily card from the *Archangel* deck, and that day I received "Creative Writing" as a message from Archangel Gabriel. I sent in my application and received a call for an interview. I was excited, but then the fears grew stronger.

During the interview, I was asked to provide a writing sample. I silently called upon Archangel Gabriel, and immediately the thought of a writing assignment I'd done almost a year back came to mind. I had a lot of doubts, but I subsequently sent it in and was hired! The first assignment I was given was equally miraculous. I was asked to review two restaurants and had no idea what to do or how to begin. However, Archangel Gabriel ensured that I was put in contact with the right people and guided me step-by-step, calming my fears and giving me confidence.

Archangel Gabriel also made sure that Bindiya was surrounded by people who encouraged her. With all the support she received, the articles came out very well and were much appreciated. She was a published writer!

Bindiya then asked Archangel Gabriel for a way to express her spirituality, and the angel gently nudged her to create a blog, again guiding her throughout. When she was too hard on herself, Gabriel sent Bindiya messages asking her to nurture her inner child and artist.

Bindiya said, "Currently there are many ideas in my pipeline, and I'm praying that I can complete the tasks I've been given. I'm not kidding when I say that as I'm writing down these marvelous experiences, I've received *another* writing assignment. If it were not for the encouragement and constant companionship of Archangel Gabriel, I don't think I'd be living my dream!"

I'm so happy for Bindiya for pursuing her dream. Being a professional writer is highly fulfilling!

⚜   ⚜

The next story is about a writing teacher who was helped by Archangel Gabriel. This is a topic that I know about from personal experience, having taught classes at the UCLA Extension Writers' Program and also my own writing classes. Every time a teacher helps a student write, that teacher is working alongside Archangel Gabriel's mission!

I've derived great joy and fulfillment from watching some of my students become successful published authors. I can only imagine the Divine joy that Archangel Gabriel must experience by encouraging and supporting writers!

Suhana Bhatia of Mumbai (Bombay), India, writes story-screenplays for television, pens features for *The Times of India* (a national newspaper), and teaches

"Writing for Media" at a local university as a guest faculty member.

Suhana loves books and painting because she adores words and colors. She also enjoys working with angels, including angel oracle cards.

While teaching her writing students, Suhana occasionally had a feeling that she hadn't given them enough help. She was teaching without a teacher's aide or textbooks, because the media-writing field was more art than science.

Because she cared about her students' learning experience, Suhana would pray and meditate before each class. She'd visualize white light around the classroom and each student, and ask Archangel Gabriel to help her communicate well to her students. Suhana was pleased that her students would leave the classroom smiling each day and tell her that she was their favorite teacher.

On the last day of the semester, Suhana had no idea what she'd teach about. She'd already covered all the topics she intended to address that semester. Suhana recalled, "I almost felt like canceling class, since I hadn't prepared anything specific. Worried that I might not contribute much that day, I asked Archangel Gabriel to help me out. I barely remember what I prayed for, but I know I needed some urgent help!"

As Suhana taught, she was inspired to help the class analyze a television script by watching the show together! They'd previously studied film scripts, and this was an inspired idea (that she credited to Gabriel's intervention) to end the class on a high note with a thorough analysis of a popular TV series' script.

Suhana's teachings flowed effortlessly that day. She explained, "I felt like someone had put words on my tongue. It turned out to be one of the most thorough sessions that semester, for all of us. Everything that I had been teaching them also fell into place neatly."

As Suhana drove home, she thanked Gabriel for being with her in the classroom and ensuring that her last class of the semester was meaningful for the students, as well as for *her*. The next day, one of the students sent a mass text to everyone, saying what an amazing class it had been.

Suhana said, "I've had times of doubt when I wondered if angels really are around me, and then an incredible day like this one happens, reassuring me of their superpowers."

Student Writers

We usually think of Archangel Uriel as the angel whom students can turn to for intellectual support. After all, Uriel is the angel of light who can switch a lightbulb on in students' minds during exams. Many students also call upon Archangel Zadkiel, who has long been regarded as the angel who assists in developing a good memory. Zadkiel helps students remember answers from their studies.

Archangel Gabriel is also a wonderful angel who can help students with any part of their schoolwork that involves writing. For example, every student is called upon to write an essay at some point, including a woman named Laura Lawson, who was helped by Archangel Gabriel in writing her college-admission essay.

Laura was trying to fill out her admission form, but felt blocked. She decided to sleep on it and was awakened by a strong sense that someone was in the room with her. Feeling safe and peaceful, Laura noticed a large glowing figure.

Laura recalled, "I saw a tall being of light, with glimmers of white and shiny gold. I received her messages as feelings within myself, like emotions of confidence, empowerment, and inspiration. The feelings conveyed were that I was on my right path, doing what I should be doing."

The next day, as Laura was driving and thinking of her experience, she wondered, *Who was that visitor?* Right then, she turned her head and glanced at a church sign that said GABRIEL. Laura said, "Somewhere deep inside me, I always *knew* it was Gabriel."

Laura was accepted to her college of choice and has now graduated. She credits Archangel Gabriel with helping her write a strong admissions essay.

I find it interesting that Laura is yet again a person who describes Archangel Gabriel as being very tall. I believe that the angel appears this way to instill confidence

and a sense of authority within the person being helped. I've also noted that none of the folks who reported having a vision of Archangel Gabriel recounted being frightened by the experience. Actually, they've all described peaceful feelings. While these feelings may be a product of euphoric recall instead of an accurate recollection, the outcomes have certainly been pleasant in each case I've heard about.

꒰   ꒱

Here's another example of a student who excelled with the brilliant help of Archangel Gabriel.

Ever since Stevi was a little girl, she'd been drawn to various forms of writing. She also enjoyed reading at a young age and wrote all sorts of poems and stories. When she was in her senior year of high school and taking classes in English, literature, and history, among others, she was responsible for many essays and exams that were crucial to the journalism career she wanted to pursue in the future. She always stressed and worried before completing these assignments and tests, though, even if she was prepared.

Because she was so focused on her studies and her physical world, Stevi had been feeling that her spiritual side was becoming more and more difficult to tap into. So she prayed for guidance, and felt the need to meditate and detox.

During her meditations, Stevi prayed for help with writing essays, and almost immediately, she felt guided to look back on spiritual books she'd read before. She reflected on my books that reminded her of Archangel Gabriel's help with journalists and teachers, and called upon Archangel Gabriel on the nights before her essay exams, as well as right before she entered the classroom to write them.

Stevi said, "As soon as I sat down, I took deep breaths to calm myself. And as soon as I began writing, an amazing force overcame me and I felt guided as I wrote. I even heard and wrote words that I wasn't familiar with, and after I walked out of the room, I had to look up their meanings! All year I didn't receive a mark lower than a *B+* for my written work, which was fantastic. I'm sure that I was helped by the beautiful presence of Archangel Gabriel and my angels, so I thank them every day!"

Everyday Forms of Writing

Even if you're not a student or aspiring to a writing career, you can still ask for and receive Archangel Gabriel's assistance with everyday forms of writing. For example, Archangel Gabriel can help you clearly and eloquently express your ideas at work when writing up reports, forms, and e-mails.

Here's a case where a woman named Soniya Kalani was helped to pen a wonderful product slogan that really paid off. Soniya told me:

My dad runs a huge manufacturing and exporting business, and one afternoon he called me urgently to come into the office to help him with a slogan for his latest product launch. As I was driving toward the office, I mentally asked for Archangel Gabriel to help me with the right slogan for this product. The moment I stepped into the boardroom, I instantly heard in my mind: *Winner's Choice.*

The minute I shared this with the company officials, it was an instant hit! I was overwhelmed with joy when I was presented with a large check just for coming up with this great slogan. I was jumping with joy! Thank you, Gabriel—I just love you.

🙰 🙰

Archangel Gabriel's guidance is practical and down-to-earth, and can be helpful anytime you need to express yourself through the written word. Many people write blogs (short for "web logs"), which are opinion editorials that appear on personal websites and social-media sites. You can ask for Gabriel's assistance in putting your feelings into words for your blogs and other opinion essays, like a woman named Maria Flynn does.

Maria feels and hears Archangel Gabriel nudging her to write blogs. She says, "My blogs are my place for healing words to come through and for me to practice my writing skills, connect with others, and eventually tell my whole story."

Ideas for blog topics flood into Maria's mind, and once when she inquired where these ideas came from, she saw visions of golden metallic orbs. (Gabriel's aura coloring is copper, very similar to gold.) Next, Maria pulled oracle cards asking who was helping her write, and each time she drew an "Archangel Gabriel" card. So she took this as a sign, and now writes blogs and Twitter tweets daily, with lots of followers who read her writings.

The archangels keep up with the times!

Personal Journaling

The angels frequently guide people to keep personal journals, as a therapeutic tool to express one's feelings and to connect with the Divine. If you've been getting this inner nudge, then please take action. Any notebook will do as a journal, although I always feel especially inspired by ones that have a beautiful cover. However, please don't let the pursuit of a beautiful journal book cause you to procrastinate your journaling work.

When you journal, you are connecting with the infinite wisdom of God's universe. You can ask for and receive answers as you write, as a woman named Joy Perino discovered.

Joy, a scriptwriting teacher, credits Archangel Gabriel with inspiring her book *It Comes*. Gabriel also helped her heal from a painful relationship.

One day, Joy was wondering why a certain woman carried a grudge against her. She decided to write the question on a piece of paper and ask Archangel Gabriel for answers and guidance. After all, Joy's Catholic-confirmation and middle name was Gabrielle, after the angel.

Joy had never before engaged in automatic writing, but was willing to give it a try. She knew the basics of the practice were to write the question and then jot down any answer that occurred to her via her thoughts, feelings, or visions.

So, Joy wrote the question to Gabriel: "Why does this woman dislike me?" Immediately, the answers came to her: the woman was very unhappy and was jealous of Joy's happiness. That made perfect sense, and helped Joy have compassion for the woman.

Archangel Gabriel helps everyone who asks for assistance, especially with their writing work. As the supreme messenger angel, Gabriel seems to enlist people to deliver messages of Divine love through their writing work.

Over the years, I've also noticed that Archangel Gabriel helps messengers of many other varieties, as we'll explore in the next chapter.

Chapter Five

CLEAR COMMUNICATION

You've just read about Archangel Gabriel's support for messengers of the written word. In this chapter, we'll explore how the archangel facilitates clear communication via the spoken word.

The iconic image of an angel with a long flowing gown and a trumpet/horn is the depiction of Archangel Gabriel bringing forth a Divine message.

Gabriel's trumpet prepares everyone to receive messages. The instrument's music clears the air and energy, brings about a pause in conversation and activity, and readies the listener to hear what the angel has to say.

Gabriel still sends messages of love, often through receptive people who unconsciously are acting as angelic messengers. Sometimes, though, Gabriel's presence and message is clearly apparent, as this next story illustrates.

Katie Comello received a message from the archangel that was initially frightening, but then turned out to be very comforting.

On Friday, January 19, 1996, 33-year-old Katie was doing dishes. She felt almost paralyzed by sadness, for no known reason. True, her father had just been released from the hospital for a minor hernia operation the day before. But he was home now, resting.

Katie said:

Then, I felt someone come up behind me—someone much taller than I was—and put their arms around me from the back and hug my chest. I could literally feel the physical presence of a body up and down my entire back and the backs of my legs. I could feel their chest on the back of my head and their arms envelop me. I do remember feeling love and comfort. However, an immediate flash of the words *I'm sorry* flew into my head. I instantly knew the meaning of this message—my father!

I turned around and "pushed" this being away from me and tried to brush off the angel's arms and presence, and said aloud, "Gabriel, if you think this was comforting, you're wrong. I don't want you to take him. I'm not ready."

It was as if an imprinted thought went into my soul that Gabriel had come to give me the news that my dad was about to die and he (she) was letting me know that I wasn't going to be alone in the process and transition. I have no idea why I addressed the being as "Gabriel" or how I got that message. It was more of an immediate feeling.

The following Tuesday, my father passed away unexpectedly on the bathroom floor. My mother found him after he had been lying there for a few hours. I drove to the house upon receiving the phone call. I sat on the floor with him, trying to remember every detail about his face. Gabriel came again, and I felt him sit down on the floor next to me. I knew this energy was the angel and not my father because it was the same energy I'd felt in my kitchen.

I felt Gabriel's energy place one arm over my shoulders and hug me from the side. Inside my mind, I "heard" the words *I'm sorry* again.

I replied, "I know you're here. I'm still not ready to lose him, but you please take care of him, okay?" I felt the love of the embrace, and I leaned into it. This time, I didn't try to push the angel away.

To this day I can still remember exactly how I felt in my kitchen. It was so real to me, and there was no mistaking that it actually happened. I still get shivers that run up my spine when I think about it, and I always acknowledge Gabriel's presence. I have no logical explanation as to how I knew it was Gabriel, except that it's just what I felt in my heart and heard in my head. And that alone brought me great comfort during a very dark chapter in my life.

꙳ ꙳

Sometimes people are surprised, upset, or doubtful that a biblical angel like Gabriel would contact everyday people in the modern world. After all, Gabriel's visitations in the Bible only involved saints. Why would this powerful angel bother with ordinary mortals and their mundane experiences?

The answer: God's love is unlimited, omnipresent, and unconditional. The Divine is also timeless. God didn't stop sending angels to us 2,000 years ago. The nameless and the famous angels are among us more

than ever before, because our complicated world needs extra protection and guidance from God's messengers.

When we remember that Gabriel is nonphysical, and therefore not limited by space or time restrictions, we can understand how the archangel can be with everyone at once. That's why we needn't worry that we're "bothering" the angels by requesting their assistance. The spiritual truth is that they are able to help everyone who calls upon them simultaneously.

Children's Connections to Angels

Children are beautifully open-minded, so they readily believe in angels. Sometimes their belief is based upon personal experiences they've had. When I was a child, I had many angel interactions, and I find that this is a common pattern among children worldwide. Many "invisible friends" are actually guardian angels.

Over the years, I've received many stories of children having interactions with archangels. The most impressive stories come from those who had no prior knowledge of these archangels, yet who accurately describe the names, specialties, and other characteristics of specific ones.

I believe that children easily connect to angels because young minds aren't filled with the skepticism or doubt that frequently plague adult minds. That's what the biblical phrase "become as little children" means, and we can all strive to have the faith of a child mixed with the knowledge of an adult.

Eight-year-old Eva* has spoken about her friend Gabriel since she was very small. Gabriel gave Eva information about future events, but she cried to her mother, Rosalie, that it was coming in too fast and intensely.

Eva told her mother that her nightly dreams were prophetic of the next day's occurrences. Eva was afraid she was creating these experiences with her dreams, and that she was a "bad person."

"It's okay, sweetheart," Rosalie reassured her crying daughter. "That doesn't mean that you're bad. That's called your *intuition*. Everyone has intuition, but some people just have it a little more than others, and it's nothing to be afraid of."

"That's what my angel said, too," Eva replied.

"An angel in your dream?" her mother asked.

"No," the little girl replied. "The angel in my room, Gabriel."

Rosalie had heard her daughter speak of her friend Gabriel for quite a while. When sharing news of family pregnancies or moves, Eva would often reply "I know— Gabriel told me." But Rosalie had always dismissed the remarks as "imaginary." To Eva, though, Gabriel was obviously very real!

Still not totally convinced of how real Gabriel actually was, however, Rosalie began to ask Eva very specific questions about the angel's appearance and visits. Eva described Gabriel as a beautiful young female angel with long brown hair and full sweeping wings. She said the angel glowed with the colors white and yellow, and often came to her along with a German-shepherd dog and other animals.

The angel's visits had become more frequent both in dreams and in waking time when Eva was in her room alone. Gabriel would tell Eva not to be afraid and that she'd be helping her on her journey to learn new things the angel had come to teach her. Gabriel would also bring Eva sweet messages from loved ones who had passed away.

With her mother's support, Eva's tears subsided while she talked of the close relationship she'd formed with her angel, Gabriel. She began to smile as she remembered the comforting words spoken to her, assuring her that the messages she heard were not "bad" and that the angel would always be by her side. Rosalie says:

"Thank you, Archangel Gabriel, for helping and comforting my daughter."

How wonderful that Eva has an understanding and gentle parent to comfort and teach her!

Too many people have told me they were punished as children for reporting their angel encounters. A few confided to me that they were hauled to psychiatrists or even psychiatric hospitals, just because they told their parents they talked to angels! I was happy to find that despite their painful experiences, they continued to believe in angels. Of course they did, because they *knew* that angels were real!

Parents do their children a huge favor by exploring the topic of angels with them. I've even written a children's book called *Thank You, Angels!* to help parents and children talk about this together. It's important to give children a safe forum to openly discuss all of their visions and spiritual experiences. Otherwise, they hold it all inside and feel disconnected from both life *and* reality.

Clear Communication

Archangel Gabriel can also strengthen the bonds between parents and children by teaching communication skills. After all, the basis of being a messenger is *clear communication*. Gabriel coaches the skill of expressing

feelings and thoughts, as a woman named Merle Tomson discovered.

For as long as Merle can remember, writing has been easy for her. On the other hand, talking in a way in which she could open her soul completely was something that she had trouble with (as a result of past situations and also as a form of protection).

Many years ago Merle's mother called her into the

kitchen to talk and drink tea. Usually, she wouldn't have been open to that type of invitation, but Merle felt so strongly that it was important to her mother that she agreed to sit down. Normally the type of communication between the two was pretty much limited to "Hi" and "Good-bye," and they'd never had deeper conversations. Merle explained:

Inside my mind, I called upon Archangel Gabriel for help, as I didn't know how to start talking to my mom. Suddenly I was really relaxed, and felt inside of me that all was well and would *be* well. I was able to talk to my mother in a way that I'd never been able to before. As I discussed my dreams and wishes, I felt a sense of amazing lightness come over me. All my words came so easily, although when I first started talking, I hadn't had any idea what I would say and where the conversation would go.

When I talked about the most important thing—how much I wanted to do my best, help others, and try to make the world a better place—I felt warmth in my heart chakra. It seemed to me as if something inside of me had opened and was being healed.

I'm pretty sure that when I finished talking, my mother must have also been feeling something amazing. She was the kind of person who always held everything inside her instead of sharing, so I think that obstacle was lifted from her shoulders.

After Merle had opened herself up to her mother completely, her mom told her things about her relationship with her father, and also related other profound thoughts and feelings that she'd never expressed before. Merle attributes the openness that arose between the two of them to her prayers to Archangel Gabriel. The relationship between mother and daughter changed profoundly from that day on.

⚞ ⚟

If, like Merle, you have difficulty opening up to others about your true feelings, call upon Archangel Gabriel for support:

"Dear God and Archangel Gabriel, please help me clearly, lovingly, and thoughtfully express my feelings to others. Help me feel confident and secure in my abilities, emotions, and opinions. Thank you for guiding my communication skills in all of my relationships. Amen."

In any relationship, it's important to be authentic and honest. This is the only way that someone else can get to know you. If you hide your feelings to please or placate another, then that other person isn't truly in a relationship with you—he or she is in one with a fictitious character! So, calling upon Archangel Gabriel for communication coaching is essential to creating healthy relationships.

Peaceful Communication

Often we are called to do the work of the angels, and bring about peace in our interactions with others.

Archangel Gabriel works through us on these occasions. Sometimes the angel may guide us to say certain helpful words or phrases. Other times Gabriel works behind the scenes to bring about peaceful resolutions. Here's an example:

Troy Schmit is what I call an "undercover lightworker" because he's a psychic medium who also works in a retail store. People such as Troy bring angelic help to these ordinary situations, and no one even knows about it!

For instance, a female customer became irate when Troy told her that he couldn't honor her expired coupon. She demanded to speak to a manager, who told her the same thing. Up the chain of command the woman went, not accepting the answer she was given. Troy

decided to call upon Archangel Gabriel to bring about peaceful communication.

Immediately, the woman calmed down, and the chief manager made a concession that allowed her to receive a discount. Everyone was happy, and Troy smiled knowingly at Gabriel's intervention.

I love Troy's story, because it shows the miraculous way in which Gabriel can deliver healing messages. As his story illustrated, you can silently ask for Gabriel to intervene in any situation. While the angel can't violate someone's free will, Gabriel's very presence has a calming effect upon everyone in the vicinity.

Business-Meeting Communication

It's not what you say, but *how* you say it that counts. Part of clear communication involves projecting your voice and energy enough to garner others' attention and respect. This is especially true in competitive business settings, where employees are jockeying for the lead position.

If you've spent any time at business meetings, you know how people can compete for attention and credit. So if you have a good idea, you'd better speak up in order to advance your career.

Archangel Gabriel can lend support to those whose intentions are pure (rather than ego based) so that their ideas are noticed and understood.

For example, a woman named Saumya used to work in the human-resources department of a college, where her role over five years ranged from giving corporate presentations to students at campuses; to discussing financial plans with department heads; to negotiating with employees and managers on policies, appraisals, and salaries.

Initially, Saumya had trouble getting her point across—being assertive at certain times, and diplomatic at others, depending on the situation. So she started

calling upon Archangel Gabriel before her meetings to request help establishing effective and harmonious communication for the highest good of all involved (she never failed to add this last part). As a result, not only did Saumya find that meetings would go unexpectedly well, but she would also be lauded for the many points she raised.

Saumya recalled, "In fact, some of my assets, as listed in my evaluation, were my communication skills and my connection with customers. I can only tell you how humbled I was to hear this. There were times when, consciously and intellectually, I felt that I'd hit a roadblock and didn't know where to go from there, so I truly rely on Archangel Gabriel for her continued love and support as I progress in my career!"

Saumya's success resulted from her following these steps:

- Asking for Archangel Gabriel's help, and asking that this help be for the highest and best good of everyone (no ego involvement on your part)

- Surrendering, or getting out of Archangel Gabriel's way (not struggling with Gabriel for power and control or rebelling against Divine guidance)

- Noticing intuitive feelings or thoughts that guide you to take positive action

- Asking God and Archangel Gabriel to give you signs that you've clearly heard and understood their guidance

- Following this guidance without delay or hesitation

Giving Speeches

According to surveys, public speaking is the biggest fear of most adults. Getting up in front of a group and talking is scarier than death, divorce, or illness, according to research. So, you're in good company if your heart thumps, your voice shakes, and your throat tightens at the thought of holding a microphone while standing in front of an audience.

Fortunately, Archangel Gabriel calms and coaches those who give speeches that bring healing messages. As a professional speaker, I've been in many situations that would ordinarily be nerve-racking. Any anxiety was defused by my prayers prior to the speech. The main message I've received before getting onstage is: "Focus upon blessing and expressing, and not upon impressing."

Angel Therapy Practitioner Kristy M. Ayala, M.A., also learned the value of praying for help with speeches. Kristy began participating in public-speaking ventures, including singing, acting, and speech competitions, when she was just seven years old. She always loved to speak in front of large audiences; it was something that just felt natural to her.

Kristy's parents realized early on that this was something she enjoyed, and they were really supportive about finding ways to foster this gift in her. So, she continued to take part in different events throughout grade school. As she got older, however, she stopped participating in a lot of these activities because her academic career became much more time-consuming for her.

Kristy eventually went to graduate school and became a university professor, teaching psychology. She loved being in an environment that allowed her to give lectures daily, but during this time in her life, she started receiving clear Divine guidance that she was no longer supposed to be working in the psychological field in a traditional way. She was being guided to walk away from

her career and begin working with people by using spiritual counseling and healing modalities instead.

It was a difficult time in some ways for her, as she wasn't sure how she'd be able to create this new career, and she was saddened by the prospect of leaving her students. However, she knew that she was supposed to make a change, and was committed to staying on her path.

After transitioning into her new career and receiving a lot of Divine intervention, Kristy underwent training as an Angel Therapist, and also trained in other healing modalities, eventually starting a private practice.

Kristy recalled:

> Even though I felt really fulfilled by the work I was doing, there was still a part of me that missed public speaking, and I realized that trying to push those feelings under the rug wasn't working for me. So I asked Archangel Gabriel for her help with my situation. I asked her to please intervene on my behalf. I said that if I was supposed to continue to teach and lecture on a larger scale and not just one-on-one, could she please give me a clear sign that I would easily understand. I also asked that, if I was meant to continue my public speaking, she please bring the right people and events to me, as I was unsure about how to move forward. I really tried to release any need for a particular outcome and let it go.
>
> About a month later, I received an e-mail from a local doctor who'd heard about me and my work and asked if I would give a two-hour lecture to his patients about reducing stress and

living a more balanced life. I was overwhelmed with happiness and gratitude because I knew this was clearly the work of Archangel Gabriel.

In subsequent weeks, I received more referrals and calls from other business owners and colleges asking me to give lectures to their employees, patients, and students! I was so happy, and it felt so great to be speaking and teaching again while also being able to talk about mind-body-spirit issues at mainstream events.

I am so grateful to Archangel Gabriel for guiding me, and graciously opening all of the doors for me to be able to do this work. I couldn't have done it without her help, support, and constant Divine intervention.

I know Kristy personally as a very loving, generous, and humble person. I'm so happy that she's giving speeches as a messenger of God's healing love. I also know that her success won't go to her head, because Kristy gives all credit to God. This is important, because the ego plays a little trick on us.

The ego tries to persuade us that we're specially gifted, unlike others. As soon as we allow it to elevate our self-opinion above other people, we disconnect from hearing the Divine voice. That's why staying humble and balanced, with healthy self-respect and high self-confidence, is essential. Love yourself, and know that everyone has gifts and carries the same potential as you do.

Workshop Presentations

Archangel Gabriel helps us overcome nervousness and clearly articulate our thoughts in personal and business settings. In fact, Gabriel brilliantly helps with *all* formats of public speaking and teaching. This includes workshops or seminars, speeches that last for more than two hours and involve audience participation.

Jenny Bryans, who teaches people about the faculties of the mind and also does angel-card readings combined with meditation, and her friend, a dancer, were talking about new ways to present the work they did. They came up with the idea of combining dancing with meditation, and within an hour, they had a location booked, advertising in the paper, and an outline for a workshop. That was on a Tuesday, and they'd decided to present the workshop on the next Sunday, since Jenny's friend was leaving for a vacation the following week.

Everything fell into place very quickly, but Jenny was

experiencing a block creating her portion of the workshop. Saturday arrived, and she was feeling a little desperate about it. That's when she remembered to call upon Archangel Gabriel for help.

Jenny remembered: "I pulled out Doreen's book *Archangels & Ascended Masters,* and found Gabriel's invocation. I set as my intention that I would be guided by the archangel as I wrote my meditations. After a few deep, centering breaths, I read the invocation out loud, letting the words and energy fill me up. After some more deep breaths, I picked up my pen and started to write. The words came pouring through me, and for most of the time, I wasn't even aware of what I was writing. I just

let Gabriel channel through me to create meditations that would be the most beneficial to the participants."

After an hour (which only felt like a few minutes), Jenny had all three meditations written. She thanked Gabriel and then asked for help presenting them the following day.

Jenny recalled: "I'm glad I did, because my friend and I changed things up right before the workshop. Even so, it all flowed easily and effortlessly. I could feel Gabriel's guidance the entire time, helping me pace the timings of my meditations and guiding my words as I spoke. The workshop went very well, and we're talking about running it again in the fall. From this experience, I have even more ideas flowing to me for workshops and presentations, and I will definitely call upon Gabriel when I'm creating them. Thank you, Archangel Gabriel, for your help and ongoing support!"

Because Gabriel is unlimited, the angel can assist everyone who asks for help in delivering messages. Just think or say, "Please guide my words and actions so that they bring blessings to everyone involved," and Gabriel will be there to help. The angels are messengers of God's love, yet they are bound by the Law of Free Will. So, unless we ask for aid, Gabriel and the other angels aren't allowed to intervene.

While it does matter what words you use when talking with other people, to an angel it's more about the intentions and energy behind the words. Therefore, it doesn't matter *how* you ask for help; what matters is that you do so.

Clearing Your Voice

Sometimes, clear communication involves more than word choice or confidence. Archangel Gabriel also helps those who have speech disorders or heavy accents.

For example, people had been telling Amanda Chappel for most of her life that she mumbled a lot, but she never really believed it until fairly recently, when she made the conscious decision to start concentrating on her throat chakra and clearly expressing herself.

Amanda said:

> I remember asking the angels for help so I could speak more clearly, because I asked them for help with most things. Shortly thereafter, I kept getting guidance to "read aloud." Since I usually read right before I went to bed when everyone else was asleep, it wasn't a problem. At first, I couldn't believe how out of breath I got after reading just a few paragraphs.
>
> Once I became a master of reading aloud fluidly, I got the guidance to "start singing." Since then, I've been singing consistently in the car, and when I'm home alone and the music is on, I can't believe how in touch I've gotten with the tone, volume, and clarity of my voice. Others have even noted that I speak much more clearly nowadays, and I know exactly whom to thank, since I see her name everywhere: it's Archangel Gabriel!

I've met some beautiful individuals who, like Amanda, felt frustrated when trying to verbally communicate with others. In my classes, I've worked with talented healers and teachers who are intimidated because English (or the main language of their country of residence) isn't their native tongue. These healers and teachers aren't doing their work, because they worry that other people won't understand them, or that they won't be able to articulate the correct words.

Those hurdles can be overcome with the help of Archangel Gabriel, as Amanda's touching story illustrates. Her story is also an example of how Gabriel's name is in itself a sign of the angel's presence. The next chapter will explore this topic in greater detail.

Chapter Six

GABRIEL'S NAME AND OTHER HEAVENLY SIGNS

The angels are neither secretive nor shy. They want us to know of their presence personally and globally. They know that when we realize they're real, we relax and feel safer and more comfortable.

In my previous books devoted to specific archangels (*The Miracles of Archangel Michael* and *The Healing Miracles of Archangel Raphael*), I discussed how they each send signs of their presence. Archangel Michael, for instance, will send helpful people who are named Michael, and Archangel Raphael will lead you to physicians named Dr. Raphael, and so forth.

So it's not surprising that Archangel Gabriel does the same. When you're actively working with Gabriel, or currently receiving this angel's help, you're likely to meet an inordinate number of people named Gabriel, Gabby, or Gabrielle. These aren't coincidental meetings. Heaven sends signs to validate your feelings and boost your faith in the Divine.

As an example, Gertrud Polonyi always knew that angels were protecting her, but clear signs of their presence started appearing around 2009. It was a difficult period of her life, and she was often asking for guidance from her angels, praying for their love.

Around this time, Gertrud starting meeting people named Gabriel, both male and female. Also, a song would frequently come on the radio that gave her a deep feeling of comfort, as if it were being played as a message for her. It turned out to be the song "Gabriel," by the band Lamb. That summer, Gertrud and her friends went to a festival, where, to their surprise, Lamb was the final band to perform. The last song they played was "Gabriel."

Gertrud recalled, "I still remember it so vividly—how the atmosphere totally changed from 1,000 people having fun, partying, and drinking to one of total oneness and spirit. It was an amazing shift, deeply spiritual. At the end of the song, the entire crowd, including me, went from clapping and cheering to chanting 'Ohm' together. This lasted for about a half hour. It was amazing, and I had tears running down my face."

Gertrud had struggled with her physical health since 2010, and things got really bad starting in 2011. One day when she was in a bookstore, she suddenly grew very dizzy, and she felt that she would black out right there.

Then she heard a voice in her head say, *It's okay. Just go and find a place where you can have a drink, and sit down and rest for a while.*

Gertrud managed to drag herself to a nearby coffee shop, and after ordering a chai tea, she sat down at a table facing a picture window looking out to the street. She was shaking and was having problems breathing, and all she could do was pray.

"Please help me, angels; please help me!" Gertrud pleaded.

A few minutes later, a large blue truck pulled up in front of the window where Gertrud was sitting, and she was astonished to see what was written on its side: in huge white letters, it spelled out GABRIEL.

"I suddenly had to laugh," Gertrud said. "I couldn't have gotten a clearer sign from Archangel Gabriel. I felt

shivers throughout my body, and I knew that she was with me. To my surprise, the dizziness simply disappeared; and I felt calm and peaceful, and finally could breathe again. I still smile when I think about how amazing the angels are, and what they must go through to manage to arrange everything so that we are at the right place at the right time so we can receive their messages and signs."

As I've mentioned, Gabriel's name in Hebrew means "the strength of God." The very vibration of the name emanates strength. So when Gertrud saw it, it not only confirmed that the angel was helping her . . . its energy boosted her own strength!

If *you* need more strength, repeat the name *Gabriel* aloud or in your mind.

A Child's Name

My research has taught me that God and our angels help us design the details of our lives prior to birth. We select the perfect gender, physical characteristics, parents, and place of birth, as well as other details that will support our life purpose. We also select the perfect first name.

Our first name definitely affects us. Behavioral and business researchers have found that people with certain first names are more likely to study math and science, while those with other names are statistically more likely to be successful executives.

However, most important of all is that you *like* your first name. If you resonate with and enjoy your name, it's like hearing a harmonious musical note. If you don't, you'll subtly cringe every time you hear it.

I believe that heaven "tells" expectant parents what name to give to their baby. This ensures that the child has the name that vibrationally is aligned with the child's life purpose. If the parents override this intuitive information—or don't hear it in the first place—the child won't like his or her name or will go through life not feeling connected to it. There'll be this sense of *That's not my real name!* Later in life, the person will likely change names.

As parents collectively become more spiritually sensitive and aware, I'm hearing more stories like this one from a woman named Lourdes Valencia:

Lourdes and her husband struggled to decide on a name for their unborn child. Then Lourdes had a clear and lucid dream in which she heard a voice say, "His name is Gabriel by me." Lourdes hadn't yet had a sonogram and didn't know the gender of the baby she carried, so she was surprised to hear the voice refer to her child with the pronoun *his*.

The next morning, Lourdes told her husband about the dream. Before she could say the name, though, her husband mentioned that he'd also awakened with a feeling about a name. So they decided to write the names on a piece of paper and show each other. When they exchanged papers, they were amazed to see they'd both written the same name: Gabriel! So that's what they called their son, born October 2002.

The angels made sure to tell both Mom *and* Dad which name would resonate with their child. Fortunately, they listened!

Also notable in this story is the fact that Gabriel's mother has a name that's connected with Mother Mary. Lourdes, of course, is the iconic location in the south of France where St. Bernadette had her vision of the Blessed Mother. Bernadette received instructions from Mother Mary to dig in the dirt, and a healing spring was revealed. Nearly 70 miracle healings have been verified involving people visiting the Lourdes spring, and many more unverified healings have been reported.

So, it's an even more beautiful story because Gabriel's mother's name is Lourdes, and Mother Mary and Archangel Gabriel are forever united.

Follow the Gabriel Name Clues

Many people who receive messages and guidance from Archangel Gabriel tell me that the angel sends them clues in the form of the name Gabriel. Here's an example from a woman named Elle:

As Elle's relationship was breaking up, she asked for and received a lot of help from Archangel Gabriel. Elle suspected that her partner was cheating on her, so she called upon Archangel Gabriel. Elle was guided to check her partner's Facebook page, where, ironically, she saw

that a woman named Gabby (which is short for Gabriel or Gabrielle) had posted flirtatious messages. When asked, Elle's partner admitted to an infidelity with Gabby.

Heartbroken, Elle once again turned to the archangel for help. Immediately she heard a song on the radio with the lyrics "Count yourself lucky she's taken him off your hands," and Elle realized that she was relieved to be done with the man.

Elle then followed her intuition to contact an old girlfriend, and was delighted to hear that she'd changed her name to Gabriel! Her friend did an oracle-card reading for Elle that reassured her further about leaving her unfaithful partner.

And the next day, Elle met a man at work whose name was—you guessed it—Gabriel.

Elle breathed a deep sigh, realizing that all of these signs from Archangel Gabriel let her know that she was watched over and protected.

Archangel Gabriel as a "Guardian Angel"

Since Gabriel is an unlimited being, the angel is able to be with everyone simultaneously without losing power or efficacy. Sometimes, archangels (including Michael, Raphael, and Gabriel) stay with certain people just as a guardian angel would do. Instead of coming and going, the archangel is stationed continuously at the person's side. This is usually because the person's life purpose is aligned with the specialty of that particular archangel.

You don't have to be special, "chosen," or saintlike to have an archangel at your side as a steady guardian. You simply need to have a Divine life mission that benefits from that archangel's support. If you ask for a particular one to stay with you, your chosen archangel will do so. Again, having an archangel guardian doesn't take away from that being's ability to help others, since archangels are supremely powerful and unlimited.

Over the years, I've met many people who have Archangel Gabriel stationed beside them. Usually, this is a person whose life purpose involves one of Gabriel's specialties: children or messenger work.

Technically, in angelology (the study of angels), a "guardian angel" and an "archangel" exist at two different vibrational frequencies. Archangels are more powerful and higher in frequency and station than guardian angels. They are the overseers or managers of guardian angels. Every person has a guardian angel, but not every person has an archangel with him or her. So when we say that an archangel is a guardian angel, we mean that the archangel is functioning as a steady guardian.

How do you know whether an archangel is with you, or the names of your guardian angels? All you need to do is ask.

Quiet your mind by closing your eyes and breathing deeply. Then say (aloud or silently):

"Guardian angels, please tell me your names."

Notice the first names that enter your mind. You might think of a name, or hear or see it. For Edgar Muñoz Olaya, the answer came in a dream.

Edgar began consciously asking for the name of his guardian angel. Soon after, he had a clear and lucid dream that answered his question!

He recalls, "I was in a big white room. Toward the back left side of the room, an angel dressed in a semi-transparent white robe was suspended in the air. This angel had short blond hair. I looked into his blue eyes, but he didn't say a word. He knew my question, though, because after a short while two other angels entered the room, moving from left to right. Each angel held a corner of a rectangular marble stone that had a name written in red letters in a font very similar to Brush Script. The name was Gabriel."

Edgar woke up very impressed and happy. It's a dream that he'll never forget.

The angels frequently answer our questions through dreams, because that's when the ego-mind (that part of us that's afraid and skeptical) is asleep. In fact, as I touched upon in Chapter 3, it's very effective to think of a question for God and your guardian angels as you're falling asleep. They'll definitely answer you during dream time. You may not remember the details when you awaken as clearly as Edgar did. However, the answer will be in your unconscious mind, where it will help guide and support your further actions.

In the next story, a woman who heard that Gabriel was her guardian received further communication in her dreams.

Patrizia was at a workshop that guided her to ask her guardian angel's name. When she heard "Gabriel," she was surprised, as she regarded the archangel as a biblical figure only. Additionally, Patrizia had been through some very tough times, which had shaken her faith.

When Patrizia returned home from the workshop and told her family about her angel experience, her ten-year-old daughter, Vanessa, who talks to angels, decided to teach her mother how to hear Gabriel's voice. Patrizia said:

> I was so blocked because of the enormous fear that was so deep within me from my childhood upbringing. At some point, I fell asleep and in my dream I could hear the voice saying, "You needn't be scared of me. I am not going to hurt you." It was the most beautiful voice I'd ever heard, because it was pure love and sounded like music. To this day, when I remember the sound of Gabriel's voice, it makes me cry.
>
> Being able to communicate with and receive messages from Archangel Gabriel has given us strength, courage, and lots of hope. It has calmed me and also allowed me the possibility of seeing the greater picture as to why things are happening around us.

A lot of people can relate to Patrizia's fears. If you were raised to believe that only religious authority figures can talk to God or angels, you may feel afraid of doing so yourself. You may worry about offending God or attracting a lower energy.

These fears are understandable, and of course, we do want to use discernment when connecting with the spirit world. That's why we focus upon God's Divine angels, including our beloved Archangel Gabriel.

Everyone is equally qualified to talk to God and the angels, and deserving of hearing their messages. I can imagine how beautiful and peaceful this world would be if we all continually prayed and followed our Divine guidance!

Archangel Gabriel helps everyone equally, including those who aren't familiar with this particular angel, as this remarkable story illustrates:

Izumi of Japan had heard about angels, but growing up she'd never learned any specifics. One day she read something that said, "If you want to know the name of your guardian angel, just ask." So Izumi did just that, and the name Gabriel popped into her mind.

Izumi had never heard of this angel before because she wasn't raised with Christmas or the "Christmas story" of the Annunciation.

Izumi recalled, "I was so surprised that I really heard the angel's name. It was the first time I experienced that angels are truly around me. This experience made me become interested in angels and want to know more about them."

Yes, Archangel Gabriel can and will help *you* right this very minute, if you ask. Your request can be something like:

"Dear God and Archangel Gabriel, thank you for guiding me to express myself clearly and honestly, with loving and articulate words that other people hear and take to heart. Please let all of my communications bring about healing and blessings to everyone. Amen."

In the next chapter, we'll explore what it means to be one of Archangel Gabriel's professional messengers.

Chapter Seven

GABRIEL'S PROFESSIONAL MESSENGERS

We've already seen how Archangel Gabriel assists writers in their work as messengers, and guides those who communicate through the spoken word. In this chapter, we'll look at other forms that messenger work can take.

I've found that anyone who inspires or teaches others can gain Archangel Gabriel's loving support. For example, artists make the world a more beautiful place and bring healing energy through their creative projects. Their artwork relays a special message.

Performing Artists as Healing Messengers

Those in the performing arts (actors, actresses, co-medians, and so forth) can be healing messengers. Their work inspires laughter, tears, and new ideas, which have therapeutic effects.

So it makes sense that Archangel Gabriel would shepherd and minister to all forms of messengers. In a way, I think of human messengers as being a part of Archangel Gabriel's heavenly team.

For example, Archangel Gabriel had consistently helped Shivani Sharma with her work as an actress, and she's never forgotten one particular night when the archangel came to her aid.

She was performing a play for six consecutive nights, and on the final night, Shivani's family and friends came to watch. Although she never felt nervous performing in front of strangers, she always got butterflies in her stomach when she knew that her loved ones were sitting in the audience. As a result, five minutes before performing an extremely intense and emotional monologue, she began to panic.

Shivani's fellow actors, who were accustomed to seeing her calm and collected while backstage, asked her what was wrong, and she told them about her nervousness and the reason behind it. They tried their best to console her, but no matter what they said, the butterflies in her stomach wouldn't subside.

Shivani remembered:

> My call time came, so I headed over to my entrance spot, just behind a curtain onstage. There were exactly two minutes until I would have to perform my monologue. My heart was

racing, and my palms began to sweat. I'm accustomed to calling out to my angels in times of desperation, so I immediately tried to think of an archangel who was associated with communication and the arts. I remembered reading about Archangel Gabriel, so I called out, "Archangel Gabriel! Please help me! I'm a nervous wreck!"

Instantly, I felt a strong presence on my right-hand side, followed by a calming sensation. I felt myself wanting to take long, deep breaths; and as I did, three words instantaneously came to my mind: *just be yourself.* I knew exactly what those words meant. Being myself meant being an actress who could do justice to the character I was portraying, without being distracted by who was in the audience. With that mind-set, I walked onstage.

Shivani delivered her monologue with a surge of confidence. Her voice was strong, clear, and stable. She was able to focus so well that she felt herself slip away, and her character took over. After the monologue when she went backstage, her fellow actors exclaimed, "Good job!" and her family and friends also congratulated her after the play.

Shivani said, "I experienced an amazing moment in my acting career, which could have been disastrous if it weren't for Archangel Gabriel! Now I don't hesitate to call upon her for help every time I perform!"

🦌   🦌

Archangel Gabriel is the ultimate agent, manager, and coach for artists who express healing messages. Over the years, I've heard stories of Gabriel helping actors and actresses secure roles and other outlets for their art. After all, healing energy and messages can be conveyed through plays, movies, and television shows.

Actress and painter Lisa Borchel knew that her life purpose was teaching and healing through art and acting. She ignored this fact during most of her early 20s because she was too afraid of being poor. But as she got older and tried other things, she had a spiritual awakening and felt that she had to go to L.A. to train with her acting coach.

Once she got to L.A., Lisa asked the angels for a sign or confirmation that she should move there permanently. The last night she was in the city, she was visiting some friends at a pub. While she was standing in line to go to the ladies' room, a Latin man walked up to her and said, "Hi, I'm Gabe." Lisa couldn't understand what he was saying, so he repeated, "I'm Gabe, as in 'Gabriel.'" Once the man took Lisa's hand, she instantly felt love and warmth and flashes of copper and white light.

Lisa said, "I still didn't know it was angel Gabriel at the time, but he then asked me if I was going to move to L.A. That was the sign I was seeking, and the next day, I began preparing to move to L.A. for good."

🐎 🐎

How many times has a play or movie inspired you or caused you to see life in a new way? Maybe you've even had your life changed by a particularly inspiring performance. This is God's healing energy being channeled through the artists' performances.

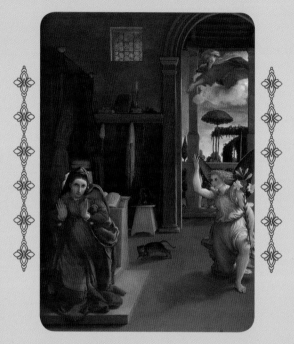

Each play, movie, or television show involves behind-the-scenes messengers who are also delivering healing information.

Rhiannon Seals, for example, works backstage at the theater, helping actors and actresses prepare for their stage performances. Rhiannon has always been clairvoyant and has received messages throughout her life. However, she learned the hard way not to share these messages with others because they weren't always well received.

One night, though, at her job Rhiannon took a chance and shared a message from Archangel Gabriel. In this way, she became a messenger of the messenger angel, and it all worked out for the best!

Rhiannon recalled what happened: "As I was backstage helping an actress get into her bulky costume, I got a high-pitched ringing sound in my right ear, which is always the sign of Gabriel's messages." Rhiannon then saw a vision of Gabriel standing behind the actress.

"I knew Gabriel had a message for me to deliver to this actress, so I proceeded cautiously. First I asked her if she believed in angels. When she said yes, I told her that Archangel Gabriel was standing behind her." Rhiannon explained how Gabriel helped messengers, including artists such as actors and actresses.

Then Rhiannon delivered Gabriel's message to the actress: "She wants to help you with auditions and getting the jobs you desire. Be fearless and bold and you will receive your reward."

As soon as Rhiannon said that, Archangel Gabriel again appeared behind the actress, giving her confidence. Rhiannon shared this vision with the actress, who cried and got goose bumps from the information.

A week later, the actress told Rhiannon, "I wanted to tell you about what happened after you shared that vision with me. I had an audition last week, and before it was my turn I thought about what you had said. I was nervous, but then I decided to just let go of all my fears and embody the fearlessness you spoke of. Well, I went out there, gave my best audition, and it felt great! And tonight I got an e-mail from the director saying I got the lead role!"

She went on to say that this was her dream part that she had always wanted. She said she felt like the message and Archangel Gabriel's assistance won her the role.

≈   ≈

Theatrical productions are collaborative projects, requiring the expertise of many people working together. Although the actors and actresses garner the most attention, it's often the behind-the-scenes crew who can make or break a production.

In all the stories I've received of Archangel Gabriel helping with performing arts, there's always a common thread of purposeful messages coming through the production. Gabriel helps all messengers who have pure intentions to help, heal, and inspire.

Performance anxiety is normal prior to any public appearance. Yet, these fears stem from the ego, who worries about disappointing the audience. The ego's focus is consistently upon the negative "what-ifs," and often these worries become self-fulfilling.

So Gabriel lifts us out of our ego so that healing messages can come through all performances. These messages not only uplift the audience, but also the person delivering them.

Trish Grunz, who is both a theater teacher/director and an active stand-up comedienne, often calls upon Archangel Gabriel prior to a performance and feels an immediate sense that all will be well. She asks for strength, and prays that the audience will enjoy her performance (or those of her students), and that during their time together they'll forget about any problems they may have.

Trish said, "The exchange of energy that results between me and the audience truly amazes me and puts me in awe, as I know that Gabriel is with me."

Visual-Artist Messengers

So far, we've examined messenger careers that involve words, either as a written piece, spoken communication, or performing arts. Yet some people deliver their messages wordlessly through visual arts.

I think we'd all agree that artwork can stir and inspire the soul. Are you like me in loving to walk through museums and art galleries? Those who can paint are expressing God's beauty with the magic of alchemy (which is why I've included many Archangel Gabriel paintings in this book). I frequently collaborate with professional artists on my oracle-card decks and book covers. All the

artists with whom I come into contact are dedicated to their art's integrity. They paint with love and purpose.

An artist named Pamela Nielsen relayed the following story to me:

> In 2003, I began painting. Several years later I came upon the book *Archangels & Ascended Masters,* and read about the angels who assist artists.
>
> As I called upon these angels, I specifically saw a mental image of Archangel Gabriel on my right-hand side. I was painting new pieces for a huge hotel project in Las Vegas at the time. As I drove to Las Vegas, I could see Gabriel traveling with me. When I began creating new pieces, I could feel and see her presence behind my right shoulder, assisting me in my creations. I actually feel her all the time in between my artistic projects. She is with me at every step of my career.

Recently, Pamela was commissioned to create a large original painting. She called on Archangel Gabriel to assist her in selecting the colors, shape, and mood of the piece so that it would connect with her clients' energy and home. The archangel always told Pamela not to worry, and that when the time was right to actually paint the piece, she would know it. Pamela has learned to trust the creative process, which comes from within. When she does paint, she uses very few brushstrokes.

"I received the piece of metal I was to paint on, on a Wednesday," Pamela said, "and on Thursday I woke up and knew it was the day to paint this piece. I was certain that Gabriel was there, and I knew that my piece would come out exactly the way I'd envisioned it. Again, I was intuitively guided as to how much paint to use on my tools and how to apply it. It came out as I'd envisioned, and my clients were thrilled. I know that Archangel Gabriel is there with me whenever I have a project to complete. I am so grateful to have her assistance, and to know that I can count on her. She is my art angel!"

                          ✍   ✍

Healing artistry can take unlimited forms. I've met people who express healing messages through photography, fashion design, jewelry making, flower arranging, dancing, interior decorating, web design, writing and performing music, and many more media. In each case, the artist holds the intention of helping the audience. The artistry is automatically imbued with the energy of this loving intention. Even though the healing effect occurs unconsciously, it is definitely received.

In order to heal people, an artist needs an audience. This is why Archangel Gabriel is involved in connecting artists and audiences, in the same way that Archangel Raphael connects healers with clients. The angels ensure that everyone who would receive blessings from the artwork is guided to find it.

For instance, Adriana Cardenas, a Colombian graphic designer with the dream of becoming a recognized artist, had done paintings for children and had also been involved in interior decorating, but she had no idea how to get in contact with galleries so that her art could be seen more widely.

Knowing that Gabriel is a very loving and powerful archangel who helps artists, she decided to call upon the messenger angel and ask that the doors of opportunity be opened for her. Adriana also decided to open her heart fully so she could receive without conditions.

A few weeks later, she was invited to an expo where people with small businesses were able to show their work. Adriana decided to participate, feeling deep inside her heart that it was a door that was opening for her.

Adriana recalled:

Many people visited the expo and came up to my booth. At one point, a man in his late 40s with very nice energy and loving words started asking me about my paintings and the techniques I was using.

After we'd talked for a while, he smiled at me and said, "I think that your work is beautiful, and you will have a bright future with your paintings. I know you will be famous with your art. My name is Gabriel, like the archangel, so you won't forget my name. I'm an architect and have a master's in fine arts, and I have all the contacts you can imagine with art galleries here in Colombia and in other countries. I would like to work with you and guide you, if you'd like me to."

I've been working with him for six months, preparing my first exhibition to be held in Toronto, Canada, in two months. And I'll be at two more exhibitions to be held soon.

What else can I say? Angels such as Gabriel are always by our side. We only need to open our hearts to receive their love with gratitude.

Once again, Archangel Gabriel left a calling card by sending a namesake person to help!

Musical Messengers

The ancient Greeks believed in music's healing power. Apollo, the god of music, was the father of Aesculapius, the god of healing. Music therapy was introduced into the hospital of Aesculapius. Plato, Pythagoras, and the Chinese sage Confucius all taught about the emotional and physical healing properties of music. In modern times, scientists have verified that music is beneficial for physical health.

Beautiful melodies and the words in songs can uplift and inspire. So it makes sense that Archangel Gabriel would assist people who deliver healing energy and loving messages through music. Just as with performing artists and writers, musicians can call upon Archangel Gabriel for guidance and support. The angel provides inspiration and motivation, along with connecting musicians to audiences who will receive healing benefits from the music.

As an example, Jacqi Maltby Michaels was blessed with the ability to make a living doing what she loves to do—sing! It has been incredibly successful at times and also very challenging. For the last decade, she's been performing a one-woman show "singing from the soul" as a headline entertainer on all the major cruise lines. She's seen the world and has made a good living, but it wasn't until she brought the angels into her work that she began to feel truly fulfilled and in Divine alignment with her purpose.

That's where Archangel Gabriel came in. A couple of years ago, the cruise industry was cutting back, and work was harder and harder to come by. Paying bills was becoming increasingly difficult, and Jacqi was also brokenhearted over the end of a relationship, so she was really struggling emotionally.

On one particular night, she was getting ready for a show and feeling so low, so unloved, and so horribly depressed. Tears filled her eyes as she put on her make-up. She had no idea how she was going to perform her high-energy one-woman show that night when she was a crumbling mess.

Jacqi recalled:

I just wanted to curl up in a ball and cry my eyes out. I told myself, *You're a pro—you can do this!* Besides, I *had* to do it because my livelihood depended on it. I stopped and prayed for help, but I was on shaky ground. I just kept putting one foot in front of the other, and I found myself backstage waiting to go on. I smiled at the stage-hands and musicians, but I was in trouble.

I went to my dressing room to pray one more time and started to fall apart again. I started calling on heaven. "I can't do this!" I screamed. "Please help me!"

Then I heard the most stunning and ethereal feminine voice say, "We will carry you. All will be well. We will carry you. You will be fine."

I asked, "Who is this?"

The response was: "I am Archangel Gabriel. I am here for you, and I will carry you. Let us do the work."

I suddenly became filled with a peaceful resolve. Almost as if I were under a spell, I walked out to the stage and began the show. As each number went by, I could feel the light growing brighter within me. When I would falter, I would clearly and lovingly hear Gabriel's voice: "Trust that we are here, and we will carry you."

Miraculously, not only did Jacqi make it through the show, but it was the best of the entire cruise. She felt Divinely inspired, and her band, the crowd, and everything else was alive with passion and excitement. After a standing ovation, she was sobbing, but this time they were tears of joy. That night she lay in bed feeling so loved and so protected, and she felt blessed to have been given such a gift. She knew then that angels were real and that they can carry you through anything!

Jacqi explained:

Ever since then, I've never gone onstage without calling on the angels to guide me and be with me during my performance. The very last thing I do before I step onstage is to ask Archangel Gabriel, *What do I need right now to best communicate God's Divine light and love to my audience?*

I always receive a one- or two-word answer, and I trust whatever it may be and carry it onstage with me. It never, ever fails me, and I come offstage knowing that I'm doing God's healing work and channeling something greater than myself. My work has become effortless and

beautiful, even when I may not be 100 percent.
Now I know why I sing!

Anyone who is committed to bringing healing messages can receive guidance and support from Archangel
Gabriel by asking for help. Just as angels are messengers
of God's healing love and light, so too can people act as
heavenly bearers of Divine inspiration.

Here's an example of a prayer you can say:

> *"Dear God, I ask for a Divine assignment to bring*
> *healing messages to anyone who needs them.*
> *May my assignment be creative and filled with joy.*
> *Thank you for your support of my artistic messages*
> *relaying your Divine love and light. Amen."*

Chapter Eight

GABRIEL, THE ANGEL OF STRENGTH

One translation of Archangel Gabriel's name is "God is my strength," and this name isn't given lightly to this powerful angel. As we've discussed throughout this book, Gabriel is a perfect balance of feminine nurturing (of parents, children, and sensitive artists) and masculine motivational power. This is probably why Gabriel is sometimes seen as female and other times as male.

For example, in the following story, Gabriel functions in a very masculine protective role, similar to Archangel Michael:

David Litterello, a business and family man from Maryland, had scheduled an important meeting in New York City. He planned on making the three-hour drive on Sunday evening so he'd be prepared to do business first thing on Monday morning.

For some reason, when he woke up on Sunday, thoughts of Archangel Gabriel went through his head, but then his day became very hectic with family activities, so he put those thoughts aside. It wasn't until about 8 P.M. that he loaded up his car and headed north to New York. Two hours into the drive, David started to get very tired. Anxious to get to his destination, he started to drive very fast. At 10:30, he was traveling about 80 miles per hour on the dark and nearly deserted New Jersey Turnpike.

As he approached the George Washington Bridge, a construction truck suddenly pulled out from the side of the highway right into the path of his car. David was groggy, so he was stunned to realize that his car seemed to make a dramatic left turn on its own, followed by a quick right turn, to avoid the oncoming truck. For the next 15 minutes, he drove in utter shock, not believing what had just occurred.

David recalled, "The whole incident seemed surreal, almost as if it hadn't happened. But then I remembered how I'd been thinking about Archangel Gabriel that morning when I woke up. I knew that only an angel could have interceded at that moment to help me avoid hitting the oncoming truck. The meeting the next day turned out to have a major impact on my career and life, and the experience changed me in many ways."

When you need strength and protection, Archangel Gabriel is there for you.

High-Tech Messenger

Although most people think of Archangel Gabriel in biblical terms, the angel has kept up with modern times. Gabriel still has a trumpet to herald messages, but also is well versed in current modes of technology. I love this story of how Gabriel showed up during a texting session:

Cherry Hsu, a New Zealand native, had an interesting encounter with Archangel Gabriel at my Angel Intuitive workshop in Australia not too long ago. During a meditation, I called out each of the archangels' names, one by one, accompanied by their corresponding melodic tunes. As soon as she closed her eyes, Cherry went into a tranquil state.

When I called out "Archangel Gabriel," Cherry saw a bright orange light in her mind's eye and instantly felt a strong connection with the archangel. Then, all of a sudden, her mobile phone started vibrating in her handbag.

Cherry said, "At the time I thought, *Thank goodness it was on silent and I didn't jump out of my chair!*"

After the meditation, Cherry checked her phone and read a text message from a friend's daughter asking for help with an IT problem. She was a bit surprised, as she rarely received any texts from this woman, but Cherry got in touch with her and was happy that she could resolve the issue.

"Later on, in hindsight," Cherry recalled, "I thought that was interesting, as Archangel Gabriel is associated with communication and the delivery of messages. It was as if Gabriel wanted to let me know of her supportive presence by literally delivering a text message from afar. In turn, I was able to be of help to my friend's daughter."

Clear Messages and Signs

If, like Cherry, you think you are getting a message from Gabriel . . . trust that you *are*. If you're still not sure if it's really a Divine message, ask for validation:

> *"Please send me a sign in the physical world that I'll easily notice and understand to help me know that I've heard you accurately."*

Or, if you're already receiving signs but are unsure what they mean, you can say:

> *"Please give me more information as to the meaning and guidance behind these symbols. Help me to know how this information applies to me."*

If you *do* know what Archangel Gabriel's guidance is, yet you're intimidated or insecure about following it, you can ask for more strength and courage:

> *"Please support my faith, strength, and courage in making healthful life changes and taking action upon the path of my Divine life purpose."*

Twists and Turns

When we ask for God's help, it's always given. Our Creator's infinite wisdom already sees the solutions to every type of problem. Usually, these solutions involve twists and turns that are beyond our human capacity to plan for or foresee.

That's why it's so important to release the need to control the outcome of your prayers. Simply pray for help, and then get out of God's way.

When you expect prayers to be answered a certain way, you may miss noticing the answer, because it shows up differently than you expect. Or, if your prayer involves "telling God how to fix things," you can slow the resolution of your situation.

After you pray, please don't waste time or energy worrying about "how" your prayer will be answered. Leave the logistics up to God.

Your only role in answered prayer is to offer up the initial request (because of the Law of Free Will, as I've mentioned before, heaven can only intervene if you give permission), and then follow any guidance you're given.

Here's a great example, from a woman who asked for new friends and then followed the guidance she received:

Kristina G. recently discovered that Archangel Gabriel is one of her guardian angels. After "writing" to the angel, telling of how she wanted to develop her photography skills and also have new friends come into her life, Kristina heard something that sounded like Morse code coming from her bedroom window. She looked out and saw a beautiful sunset and was inspired to go outside and take photos of it.

Kristina said:

> As I was taking pictures, a girl walking her dog came by. We talked for a bit, then she continued walking. A voice said to me, "Talk to her," over and over again. I ran after the girl telling her to wait. I talked to her some more and got

her phone number. We're planning on getting to know each other, and we're going to hang out!

About an hour after that, I found out that one of my favorite nature photographers was of-

fering a forum for people to share their ideas and develop their work. I can't wait to be a part of it! I'm so grateful to God and the angels for their love, guidance, and support.

Kristina had both of her requests (photography and friendship) fulfilled at the same time, because she was willing to follow her inclination to go outside, talk with a stranger, and join a photography club. Following guidance sometimes takes us out of our comfort zone, but it's always worth it.

Gabriel, the Down-to-Earth, Practical Angel

Some people think of angels as "airy-fairy" beings, yet they are entirely practical. Angels are here to enact God's mission of peace, one person at a time. So, angels are happy to help you and your loved ones with whatever brings *you* peace. And that's a *very* practical mission!

Archangel Gabriel will assist with communication of all forms, as we've seen in the examples throughout this book. Since clear communication is the basis of both personal and business relationships, Archangel Gabriel heals our connections with others by guiding our spoken and written words.

That's why it makes sense that Archangel Gabriel intervened in an insurance-settlement situation so that clear communication could prevail:

Years ago, Lamdany's 13-year-old daughter, B.*, was involved in a terrible accident on her way home from school. She was hit by a truck, and it was a miracle that she survived. It took almost a year and a half before she could walk again. The family thought that everything was okay, and that life could return to normal, but after a while, B. started feeling more and more pain, and after four years of walking, she needed her crutches again. Four years after that, she was in a wheelchair. Nobody could explain that kind of regression.

Meanwhile, the insurance company responsible for the long-term care after school accidents refused to pay because they believed that there must have been a new reason that B. couldn't walk anymore after so much time.

Nothing seemed to be going in a positive direction. B. fell from her wheelchair, hurting her arm, she went into a severe depression, and she needed to take psychotropic drugs.

Lamdany recalled:

> In the summer of 2008, I read in one of Doreen's books that Archangel Gabriel is the one who can help when there's a block in a situation, so I begged Gabriel for help to heal all the causes that prevented a positive outcome in my daughter's situation. A few days later, I had a relieved feeling about the whole thing. I felt quite sure for the first time that everything would work out someday.
>
> Weeks later, B. sent us an e-mail from college, where she was studying physics, and asked us if it would be okay to go to a rehabilitation clinic to get some help for her arm. Of course we told her to go there as soon as possible even though the insurance company refused to pay for it.
>
> At that clinic, B. met a fellow patient who struck up a conversation with her. It turned out that he was the vice president of the insurance company that had refused to help her. He then set up a meeting at the company so that she could get some financial assistance.
>
> My husband and I joined B. at the meeting, and the vice president from the insurance company was there. The first thing he did was to

apologize to our daughter for everything she had to bear because of the mistakes made by his company. She ended up getting reimbursed not only for previous medical expenses, but also enough to pay for her rehab at the clinic.

For everyone involved, this was a miracle, and it all just happened to occur a few days before Christmas. Lamdany and her family thanked the vice president profusely for his help, and of course, expressed gratitude to Archangel Gabriel for this Divine intervention.

You Know Archangel Gabriel Is With You When . . .

Gabriel, like all the archangels, is unconditionally loving, nondenominational, and unlimited, and looks past the surface and sees your true Divine nature and life purpose. So Gabriel is delighted to help you—and everyone—with situations involving children, clear communication, and the need for strength.

All it takes is your request. Just think or say the name *Gabriel,* and the angel is instantly there by your side. Like the other archangels, Gabriel's presence is unmistakable. You know Archangel Gabriel is with you when you . . .

- • . . . have a sudden out-of-the-blue thought about Archangel Gabriel.

- • . . . keep hearing or reading references to Gabriel.

- • . . . keep meeting people named Gabriel.

- • . . . have a sudden strong desire to write.

- • . . . make a commitment to working on your artistic projects.

- . . . receive intuitive messages about your child.

- . . . have a strong desire to help children.

- . . . see the color copper or orange everywhere you go, or you're attracted to these colors.

- . . . see sparkling flashes of copper or orange light, without any physical origin.

- . . . see white lilies.

- . . . see bugle horns or trumpets.

- . . . *feel* that Gabriel is with you.

Children naturally trust their intuition, including their feelings about angels. My prayer is for adults to retain this pure faith.

When Rolinka was four years old, her father gave her an angel Christmas ornament. Little Rolinka immediately decided it was Archangel Gabriel, even though her family didn't understand her reasoning. Since that day, Rolinka has talked to Gabriel about everything, which was a relief for this lonely little girl who never felt like she fit in with other people.

Rolinka knows that Gabriel is counseling and comforting her. She does her best to listen, especially while going through life changes or painful experiences. At age 47, she still has her Gabriel ornament.

Rolinka mentioned one other sign that the angels (including Gabriel) are communicating with you: a high-pitched ringing sound or beep in one ear. This is the non-verbal way that angels "download" important information to you. You may not hear their specific words, but their answers will be there as a knowingness in your mind.

The ear in which you hear this ringing or beeping sound is your "spirit ear," and you can trust the sounds you receive there. Conversely, the other ear is usually the "ego ear," which gives you worrisome thoughts based upon fear instead of reality. Once you begin to distinguish between these ears, you'll develop even more faith in the presence of the Divine.

You can also ask that the ringing or beeping sound be lowered to a softer volume, if it's too loud. And the best news of all is that you can ask Archangel Gabriel to speak up, if needed, or to clarify any confusing message.

All you have to do is ask!

❧   ❧   ❧

ZDRAVO·MARIJO·MILOSTI·PUNA

Fec et pi
Collegium
Sušilov

Appendix

Biblical References to Archangel Gabriel

These are the passages from the King James Version of the Bible in which Gabriel is specifically named:

And I heard a man's voice between the banks of Ulai, which called, and said, Gabriel, make this man to understand the vision.

(Daniel 8:16)

Yea, whiles I was speaking in prayer, even the man Gabriel, whom I had seen in the vision at the beginning, being caused to fly swiftly, touched me about the time of the evening oblation.

(Daniel 9:21)

Forasmuch as many have taken in hand to set forth in order a declaration of those things which are most surely believed among us,

Even as they delivered them unto us, which from the beginning were eyewitnesses, and ministers of the word;

It seemed good to me also, having had perfect understanding of all things from the very first, to write unto thee in order, most excellent Theophilus,

That thou mightest know the certainty of those things, wherein thou hast been instructed.

There was in the days of Herod, the king of Judaea, a certain priest named Zechariah, of the course of Abia: and his wife was of the daughters of Aaron, and her name was Elisabeth.

And they were both righteous before God, walking in all the commandments and ordinances of the Lord blameless.

And they had no child, because that Elisabeth was barren, and they both were now well stricken in years.

And it came to pass, that while he executed the priest's office before God in the order of his course,

According to the custom of the priest's office, his lot was to burn incense when he went into the temple of the Lord.

And the whole multitude of the people were praying without at the time of incense.

And there appeared unto him an angel of the Lord standing on the right side of the altar of incense.

And when Zechariah saw him, he was troubled, and fear fell upon him.

But the angel said unto him, Fear not, Zechariah: for thy prayer is heard; and thy wife Elisabeth shall bear thee a son, and thou shalt call his name John.

And thou shalt have joy and gladness; and many shall
rejoice at his birth.

For he shall be great in the sight of the Lord, and
shall drink neither wine nor strong drink; and he
shall be filled with the Holy Ghost, even from his
mother's womb.

And many of the children of Israel shall he turn to the
Lord their God.

And he shall go before him in the spirit and power
of Elias, to turn the hearts of the fathers to the
children, and the disobedient to the wisdom of the
just; to make ready a people prepared for the Lord.

And Zechariah said unto the angel, Whereby shall I
know this? for I am an old man, and my wife well
stricken in years.

And the angel answering said unto him, I am Gabriel,
that stand in the presence of God; and am sent
to speak unto thee, and to shew thee these glad
tidings.

And, behold, thou shalt be dumb, and not able to
speak, until the day that these things shall be
performed, because thou believest not my words,
which shall be fulfilled in their season.

And the people waited for Zechariah, and marvelled
that he tarried so long in the temple.

And when he came out, he could not speak unto them:
and they perceived that he had seen a vision in the
temple: for he beckoned unto them, and remained
speechless.

And it came to pass, that, as soon as the days of his
ministration were accomplished, he departed to his
own house.

And after those days his wife Elisabeth conceived, and
hid herself five months, saying,

Thus hath the Lord dealt with me in the days wherein he looked on me, to take away my reproach among men.

And in the sixth month the angel Gabriel was sent from God unto a city of Galilee, named Nazareth,

To a virgin espoused to a man whose name was Joseph, of the house of David; and the virgin's name was Mary.

And the angel came in unto her, and said, Hail, thou that art highly favoured, the Lord is with thee: blessed art thou among women.

And when she saw him, she was troubled at his saying, and cast in her mind what manner of salutation this should be.

And the angel said unto her, Fear not, Mary: for thou hast found favour with God.

And, behold, thou shalt conceive in thy womb, and bring forth a son, and shalt call his name JESUS.

He shall be great, and shall be called the Son of the Highest: and the Lord God shall give unto him the throne of his father David:

And he shall reign over the house of Jacob for ever; and of his kingdom there shall be no end.

Then said Mary unto the angel, How shall this be, seeing I know not a man?

And the angel answered and said unto her, The Holy Ghost shall come upon thee, and the power of the Highest shall overshadow thee: therefore also that holy thing which shall be born of thee shall be called the Son of God.

And, behold, thy cousin Elisabeth, she hath also conceived a son in her old age: and this is the sixth month with her, who was called barren.

For with God nothing shall be impossible.

And Mary said, Behold the handmaid of the Lord; be it unto me according to thy word. And the angel departed from her.

And Mary arose in those days, and went into the hill country with haste, into a city of Juda;

And entered into the house of Zechariah, and saluted Elisabeth.

And it came to pass, that, when Elisabeth heard the salutation of Mary, the babe leaped in her womb; and Elisabeth was filled with the Holy Ghost:

And she spake out with a loud voice, and said, Blessed art thou among women, and blessed is the fruit of thy womb.

And whence is this to me, that the mother of my Lord should come to me?

For, lo, as soon as the voice of thy salutation sounded in mine ears, the babe leaped in my womb for joy.

And blessed is she that believed: for there shall be a performance of those things which were told her from the Lord.

And Mary said, My soul doth magnify the Lord,

And my spirit hath rejoiced in God my Saviour.

For he hath regarded the low estate of his handmaiden: for, behold, from henceforth all generations shall call me blessed.

For he that is mighty hath done to me great things; and holy is his name.

And his mercy is on them that fear him from generation to generation.

He hath shewed strength with his arm; he hath scattered the proud in the imagination of their hearts.

He hath put down the mighty from their seats, and
exalted them of low degree.

He hath filled the hungry with good things; and the
rich he hath sent empty away.

He hath holpen his servant Israel, in remembrance of
his mercy;

As he spake to our fathers, to Abraham, and to his seed
for ever.

And Mary abode with her about three months, and
returned to her own house.

Now Elisabeth's full time came that she should be
delivered; and she brought forth a son.

And her neighbours and her cousins heard how the
Lord had shewed great mercy upon her; and they
rejoiced with her.

And it came to pass, that on the eighth day they
came to circumcise the child; and they called him
Zechariah, after the name of his father.

And his mother answered and said, Not so; but he shall
be called John.

And they said unto her, There is none of thy kindred
that is called by this name.

And they made signs to his father, how he would have
him called.

And he asked for a writing table, and wrote, saying, His
name is John. And they marvelled all.

And his mouth was opened immediately, and his
tongue loosed, and he spake, and praised God.

And fear came on all that dwelt round about them: and
all these sayings were noised abroad throughout all
the hill country of Judaea.

And all they that heard them laid them up in their
hearts, saying, What manner of child shall this be!
And the hand of the Lord was with him.

And his father Zechariah was filled with the Holy
Ghost, and prophesied, saying,

Blessed be the Lord God of Israel; for he hath visited
and redeemed his people,

And hath raised up an horn of salvation for us in the
house of his servant David;

As he spake by the mouth of his holy prophets, which
have been since the world began:

That we should be saved from our enemies, and from
the hand of all that hate us;

To perform the mercy promised to our fathers, and to
remember his holy covenant;

The oath which he sware to our father Abraham,

That he would grant unto us, that we being delivered
out of the hand of our enemies might serve him
without fear,

In holiness and righteousness before him, all the days
of our life.

And thou, child, shalt be called the prophet of the
Highest: for thou shalt go before the face of the
Lord to prepare his ways;

To give knowledge of salvation unto his people by the
remission of their sins,

Through the tender mercy of our God; whereby the
dayspring from on high hath visited us,

To give light to them that sit in darkness and in the
shadow of death, to guide our feet into the way of
peace.

And the child grew, and waxed strong in spirit, and was
in the deserts till the day of his shewing unto Israel.

(Luke 1)

About the Author

Doreen Virtue holds B.A., M.A., and Ph.D. degrees in counseling psychology and works with the angelic realm. She is the author of the *Healing with the Angels* book and oracle cards; *Archangels & Ascended Masters;* and *The Angel Therapy® Handbook,* among other works. Her products are available in most languages worldwide.

Doreen has appeared on *Oprah,* CNN, *The View,* and other television and radio programs, and writes regular columns for *Woman's World* and *Spirit & Destiny* magazines. For more information on Doreen and the workshops she presents, please visit: **www.AngelTherapy.com.**

You can listen to Doreen's live weekly radio show, and call her for a reading, by visiting **HayHouseRadio.com®**.

✎   ✎   ✎

Hay House Titles of Related Interest

YOU CAN HEAL YOUR LIFE, *the movie,*
starring Louise L. Hay & Friends
(available as a 1-DVD program and an expanded 2-DVD set)
Watch the trailer at: **www.LouiseHayMovie.com**

THE SHIFT, *the movie,*
starring Dr. Wayne W. Dyer
(available as a 1-DVD program and an expanded 2-DVD set)
Watch the trailer at: **www.DyerMovie.com**

✒   ✒

ACTIVATE YOUR GOODNESS: *Transforming the World Through Doing Good*, by Shari Arison

ALL IS WELL: *Heal Your Body with Medicine, Affirmations, and Intuition,*
by Louise L. Hay and Mona Lisa Schulz, M.D., Ph.D.

IS: *Your Authentic Spirituality Unleashed*, by Faith Freed

MESSAGES FROM MARGARET: *Down-to-Earth Angelic Advice for the World . . . and You*, by Gerry Gavin

THE RADICAL PRACTICE OF LOVING EVERYONE: *A Four-Legged Approach to Enlightenment,*
by Michael Chase

WISHES FULFILLED: *Mastering the Art of Manifesting,*
by Dr. Wayne W. Dyer

All of the above are available at your local bookstore,
or may be ordered by contacting Hay House (see next page).

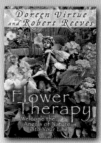

We hope you enjoyed this Hay House book. If you'd like
to receive our online catalog featuring additional information
on Hay House books and products, or if you'd like to find
out more about the Hay Foundation, please contact:

Hay House, Inc., P.O. Box 5100, Carlsbad, CA 92018-5100
(760) 431-7695 or (800) 654-5126
(760) 431-6948 (fax) or (800) 650-5115 (fax)
www.hayhouse.com® • www.hayfoundation.org

Published and distributed in Australia by: Hay House Australia Pty.
Ltd., 18/36 Ralph St., Alexandria NSW 2015 • *Phone:* 612-9669-4299
• *Fax:* 612-9669-4144 • www.hayhouse.com.au

Published and distributed in the United Kingdom by: Hay House
UK, Ltd., Astley House, 33 Notting Hill Gate, London W11 3JQ
Phone: 44-20-3675-2450 • *Fax:* 44-20-3675-2451
www.hayhouse.co.uk

Published and distributed in the Republic of South Africa by:
Hay House SA (Pty), Ltd., P.O. Box 990, Witkoppen 2068 • *Phone/Fax:*
27-11-467-8904 • www.hayhouse.co.za

Published in India by: Hay House Publishers India, Muskaan
Complex, Plot No. 3, B-2, Vasant Kunj, New Delhi 110 070 • *Phone:*
91-11-4176-1620 • *Fax:* 91-11-4176-1630 • www.hayhouse.co.in

Distributed in Canada by: Raincoast, 9050 Shaughnessy St.,
Vancouver, B.C. V6P 6E5 • *Phone:* (604) 323-7100
Fax: (604) 323-2600 • www.raincoast.com

Take Your Soul on a Vacation

Visit **www.HealYourLife.com®** to regroup, recharge,
and reconnect with your own magnificence.
Featuring blogs, mind-body-spirit news, and
life-changing wisdom from Louise Hay and friends.

Visit **www.HealYourLife.com** today!